Destination *Alchemy*

Publisher	Austin Wilde
Artistic & Creative Director	Gina Wilde
Editor & Production Manager	Sandi Rosner
Graphic Design & Layout	Eric Youngquist
Schematics	Shiri Mor
Photography	Kathryn Martin
Fashion Stylist	Gina Wilde
Hair and Make-up	Kira Lee
Models	Tessa Grul, Irma Spars, Sarah McPherson and Cameo LeBrun

⊕ ALCHEMY
YARNS OF TRANSFORMATION

Alchemy Yarns of Transformation
P.O. Box 1080
Sebastopol, CA 95473

www.alchemyyarns.com
alchemyyarns@pacbell.net

ISBN: 9780980105704

Printed in China

First Printing January 2008
10 9 8 7 6 5 4 3 2 1

Special thanks to:

Dressers, 141 N. Main St, Sebastopol, CA, for
providing wardrobe for the photo shoot.

Jamie Murray Surfboards. Visit Jamie online at
http://www.headhighglassy.blogspot.com to
learn more about his cool hand-crafted boards.

Jan Webber, for designing and tooling the exquisite
leather saddlebags worn by the donkeys of Alchemy.

Making a book requires the talent and dedication
of many people, not all of whom get a listing in the
credits. **We offer our deepest gratitude to:**

La Familia Alchemia of sample knitters whose
speed and passion for beautiful fiber produced
the lovely garments in the photos: Cathi Arfin, Pat
Hellhake, and the various designers.

Clara Cabrera and **Irma Hernandez de Perez** for
their kind hearted devotion to keeping the Alchemy
Studio and Farm alive with laughter and love.

Alchemy Retailers worldwide, who share our work
with their audiences, and inspire us to continue
creating meaningful designs and beautiful yarns.

Our families, especially our collective children, **Clio,
Dylan, Joe, Emma,** and **Peanut** for their patience
and understanding while we were deep in the
process of making this book.

savor the journey, but prefer it to serve the product as well. I guess, like many of you, I'm just a regular "I'll have my cake and eat it, too" knit enthusiast.

This travel guide is an intersection of process and product. The patterns, for the most part, relax into the rightness of knitting the meditative knit, a study in beautiful fiber and exquisite color. With clear instruction, helpful tips, and classic silhouettes, the pieces in Destination Alchemy provide the ultimate knit experience, balancing the lovely act of knitting with the much-desired outcome of a beautiful creation made by the sojourner.

Gina and Austin Wilde with Daisy at the Alchemy farm

Take a trip with Alchemy. Embark on this exciting journey. We will be your guide for selecting exquisite fiber, gorgeous color, and contemporary design. May all your destinations be filled with equal parts excitement, relaxation, and new understanding. May this journey evoke the best associations of a lively adventure, bringing you a bit closer to something

authentic and deeply satisfying. May you have a delightful experience of the destinations made possible by exploring a beautiful knitting path.

Gina Wilde
Artistic and Creative Director
Alchemy Yarns

A Journey of Passion

At Alchemy Yarns of Transformation, we are passionate about everything we do. As creators of the world's finest luxury hand paint yarns, and as an innovative contemporary design house, we are committed to providing unsurpassed quality to the avid fiber arts enthusiast. Our goal is to synthesize the elements needed to offer the most extraordinary and satisfying knitting experience available.

Alchemy Yarns

Clara Cabrera, our studio manager, having a blue day

Combining time-honored Fine Art techniques, the highest quality custom-blended noble fibers, and a reverence for Nature's palette, we create yarns—and thereby opportunities for creative expression—that transcend the typical. We do not use any chemicals in dying our fiber. Only natural mordents are used in applying color to the yarns, and all dyes are environmentally friendly and 100% non-toxic. Simply put, our fibers are designed to please the senses, soothe the soul, and honor the earth.

Alchemy Designs

As a design house, we create templates for beautiful and unique knitwear, with an emphasis on the architectural adage of "form follows function." Our designs mindfully embrace a balance of process (an enjoyable and satisfying knit, with an emphasis on relaxing into the beautiful unfolding of extraordinary color and texture) and product (fashion-forward silhouettes that create very wearable works of art). Our designs are

meant to engage the creative potential in every knitter, and offer clear, step-by-step guidance to ensure a successful and enjoyable knitting journey.

The Alchemist's Way

Nestled in the beautiful rolling hills of Sonoma County, our Northern California studios and farm blend with the surrounding orchards and vineyards. Here in this pastoral setting our work family practices the art of creating exquisite hand paint yarns. Each skein is thoughtfully and artistically painted, then steamed over an open fire. We hang our yarns from bamboo rods suspended across our land, thereby allowing skeins to be dried by the cooling breezes of the nearby Pacific Ocean. Our design team is composed of smart knitters from around the world, all of whom are committed to facilitating other knitters' creative processes in the most logical and intuitive manner possible.

At Alchemy, we believe that our commitment to living life to its fullest—to recognizing and celebrating health, healing, love and light at every opportunity—is captured in each skein of yarn and every design we make. By creating our work with such intent, we trust this beauty is given over to you when you choose our fiber and design in support of your creative expression.

We invite you to share our passion.

Daisy lends a helping hoof

Welcome to the world of Alchemy

the *Tides Scarf*

by Lauren Lax

At sail on the high seas, salt air and soothing breezes lift the traveler's spirit. Each day the sun rises and sets seamlessly, bathing the elegant ship as she cuts an ocean path to lands unknown. The rest of the world is left in her wake, as mystery and adventure await the sojourner. Stand on the bow and peer into the depths of the endless horizon.

The Tides Scarf is an exercise in pure luxury. Double-stranding Silk Purse and Haiku, the rippling motif knits up in a flash, providing a rhythmic and deeply satisfying knit. Wear it wide like a shawl, or double it over for a super-warm and incredibly practical scarf!

Approx 8½" x 44"

materials

**2 skeins
Alchemy Yarns Silk Purse
Shown in 30w – Spruce**

**1 skein
Alchemy Yarns Haiku
Shown in 18c – The Night Air**

US size 10 (5 mm) needles
(or size needed to obtain gauge)

gauge

16 sts and 10 rows = 4"
*in pattern stitch with 2 strands
of yarn worked together*

Note

*This scarf is made
with one strand of
each yarn held
together throughout.*

Directions

With one strand of
Silk Purse and one of
Haiku held together,
CO 33 sts.

Rows 1 and 2: K

Row 3 (RS): K1, *k5,
yo, k1, yo2, k1, yo3,
k1, yo2, k1, yo, repeat
from * to last 5 sts, k5.

Row 4 (WS): K, working
into each group of
yarnovers only once
and dropping loops
from extra yarnovers
off needle.

Rows 5 and 6: K

Row 7: K1, *yo, k1,
yo2, k1, yo3, k1, yo2,
k1, yo, k5, repeat from
* to last 5 sts, yo, k1,
yo2, k1, yo3, k1, yo2,
k1, yo, k1.

Row 8: K, working
into each group of
yarnovers only once
and dropping loops
from extra yarnovers
off needle.

Repeat rows 1–8 for
44" or desired length.
BO all sts loosely.

FINISHING

Weave in ends. Block
lightly to size, stretching
lengthwise to open up
the pattern.

Snake Cable Camisole

by Gina Wilde

India is said to be a litmus test for travelers—some are all too happy to leave while others choose to stay a lifetime. With the motto *"Truth Alone Triumphs,"* India is bound by the Bay of Bengal to the east, the Indian Ocean on the south, and the Arabian Sea on the west. For centuries this diverse subcontinent has been home to historic trade routes and vast empires. A pluralistic, multi-ethnic, and multi-lingual land, India evokes a generous feast of color and spice in a land of extremes.

Sexy, Sultry and Sensuously Soft, the Snake Cable Camisole is knit with elegant Silk Purse, with a tantalizing back panel of sinuous cables. Make a statement coming and going in this homage to color and charm.

finished size

Chest: 34 (36, 38, 40, 42)"

materials

3 (3, 3, 4, 4) skeins
Alchemy Yarns Silk Purse
Shown in 65e – Dragon

US size 6 (4.25 mm) needles
(or size needed to obtain gauge)

Cable needle

Crochet hook

gauge

20 sts and 30 rows = 4" in St st

I-cord

Knit all sts, * slide the work to the opposite end of the needle, bring yarn around behind sts, and knit them again from the same direction. Working yarn is pulled from the last st to the first st each time a new row is started. Repeat from * for as many rows as needed.

Snake Cable Pattern

Chart columns: 10 9 8 7 6 5 4 3 2 1
Chart rows (right side): 1 3 5 7 9 11 (odd) and 2 4 6 8 10 12 (left side)

- **purl**
  RS: purl stitch
  WS: knit stitch

- **knit**
  RS: knit stitch
  WS: purl stitch

- **cable 2 over 2 right**
  RS: sl 2 to CN, hold in back. k2, k2 from CN

- **cable 2 over 2 left**
  RS: sl 2 to CN, hold in front. k2, k2 from CN

Note: Repeat sts 1–7 to last 3 sts, end with sts 8–10.

12" or desired length

6 (6, 6½, 7, 7)"

11 (12, 13, 13, 14)"

17½ (18, 19, 20, 21)"

11 (12, 13, 13, 14)"

14½ (16, 17½, 18¾, 20)"

Directions

BACK

CO 77 (84, 91, 98, 105) sts.

Row 1 (RS): P 2, work Snake Cable Pattern to last 2 sts, end P 2.

Row 2 (WS): K2, work Snake Cable Pattern to last 2 sts, k 2.

Cont in pattern as established until piece measures 2 (2, 2, 2, 2)", ending with a RS row.

Next row (Dec Row – WS): K 2, SSK, work in pattern to last 4 sts, k2tog, k 2.

Cont without shaping until piece measures 3 (3, 3, 3, 3)".

Repeat Dec Row – 73 (80, 87, 94, 101) sts.

Cont without shaping until piece measures 12 (13, 14, 14, 15)". BO in pattern.

FRONT

CO 92 (94, 96, 98, 100) sts.

Work in St st for 2 (2, 2, 2, 2)", ending with a WS row.

Next row (Dec Row – RS): K 2, SSK, k to last 4 sts, k2tog, k 2.

Cont without shaping until piece measures 3 (3, 3, 3, 3)".

Repeat Dec Row – 88 (90, 92, 94, 96) sts.

Cont without shaping until piece measures 12 (13, 14, 14, 15)", ending with a WS row.

Shape armholes and neck: Dec 1 st at beg and end of every RS row 5 times – 78 (80, 82, 84, 86) sts. P one row.

Divide for neck: Dec 1, k 36 (37, 38, 39, 40) sts, BO 2 for center front neck, attach a new ball of yarn and k to last 2 sts, dec 1 at end – 74 (76, 78, 80, 82) sts. Working both sides at once, dec 1 st side edge and 1 st at neck edge on each side every RS row until 4 sts rem on each side.

I-Cord Straps: Place one set of 4 sts on holder. With other set of 4 sts, make an I-Cord approx 12" long. Return sts to holder until you determine the exact length needed for a comfortable fit. Repeat for second strap.

FINISHING

Sew side seams.

Neck, armhole, and bottom borders: With crochet hook, work one row single crochet around all edges.

Attach straps: Try on the camisole and determine optimal length for straps. K a few more rows or rip out a few rows if needed, then BO. Attach straps to inside of garment just inside the second cable from side seam.

Weave in ends. Block lightly to size if desired. We recommend steaming on wrong side of work, using pressing cloth and being careful not to drag the iron or allow it to remain in one spot.

the *Illusionist*

by Olga Pobedinskaya

Some journeys are made to nearby ports, while others are close in proximity to the heart. And some of our most grand adventures find us never leaving the privacy of our own inner sanctum. In this landscape, dreams and fantasy become an integrated part of who we are and how we experience the world. Sometimes the real world and the realm of illusion blur, and there are moments when it may be unclear which is which.

This is the world of The Illusionist.

Texture and color know no limits in this remarkable design, knit in the irresistible Haiku. Worked lengthwise on the needle and seductively rippled with movement and drama, the knit is an exploration of simple and satisfying ruching. The Illusionist is meant to subtly unveil your full knit magic.

finished size

Approx 14" x 60"

materials

4 skeins Alchemy Yarns Haiku shown in 25c – Aubergine

24" circular US size 10 (6 mm) needle
(or size needed to obtain gauge)

Tapestry needle

gauge

18 sts and 36 rows = 4" in Slip Stitch Ribbing

Slip Stitch Ribbing

(worked on even number of sts)
Row 1: * sl 1 with yarn in front, k 1, repeat from * to end of row.
Repeat this row.

Note

The shawl is made in stripes of slip stitch ribbing alternated with St st ruches.

Directions

Loosely CO 270 sts.

Rows 1–18: Work in Slip Stitch Ribbing.

Row 19 (inc row): K in the front and back of every stitch – 540 sts.

Rows 20–29: Beginning with a purl row, work in St st.

Row 30 (dec row): * p2tog, k2tog, repeat from * to end of row – 270 sts.

Repeat these 30 rows 4 times more, then repeat rows 1–18 once.

BO loosely in ribbing.

FINISHING

Make pleats in the St st sections by using a tapestry needle and yarn to sew the increase row to the decrease row in randomly placed sections about 3" long. Keep the pleats a few inches away from the edges.

Weave in ends.

the *Surfer*
by Gina Wilde

No trip to California is complete without a visit to the Pacific Ocean—be it peaceful Zuma Beach in Southern California, a breathtaking roadtrip along Highway 1, or a perfect vista overlooking the splendor of Carmel up north. All along the stunning West Coast, surfers are working those waves, living in the moment of exhilarating opportunity.

With surfing, as in life, timing is everything.

The Surfer epitomizes West Coast cool. Inspired by the legendary Dogtown skateboarders of Venice Beach circa 1976, the unisex shirt offers laid-back easy-to-wear style. Knit from Silken Straw, with the fiber held double throughout, the piece is worked in a satisfying knit from sleeve to sleeve. This technique makes possible the relaxing yet dynamic experience of several colors unfolding in an uncomplicated way, and at the same time, gives the flattering color flash made possible only by long, uninterrupted lines of vertical color.

finished size

Chest: 34 (38, 42, 46)"

materials

Alchemy Yarns Silken Straw
6 (7, 8, 10) skeins total
in 5 different colors:

A 78c – Pablo's Solace • 1 (1, 1, 2) skeins
B 12w – Ocean Floor • 2 (2, 3, 3) skeins
C 42m – Silver • 1 (1, 1, 1) skein
D 28w – Teal Tide • 1 (1, 1, 2) skeins
E 23e – Good Earth • 1 (2, 2, 2) skeins

2 US size 7 (4.5 mm)
24" to 32" circular needles
(or size needed to obtain gauge)

US size E (3.5 mm) crochet hook

Darning needle

gauge

20 sts and 28 rows = 4"
in St st with yarn held double

Seed Stitch

(worked on ODD number of sts):
All rows: *K1, p1;
repeat from * to last st, k1.

Stripe Sequence

Label		# of Rows
Includes first 6 rows Seed St border	A	8
	B	2
	C	6
Note: If only one number appears, it applies to all sizes	B	4
	D	2
	E	12
	B	2
	A	2
Start underarm shaping on 3rd row of this stripe	C	4
	D	10
Start side shaping on 3rd row of this stripe	E	8 (22, 22, 22)
	C	2
	B	6 (6, 22, 22)
	A	14 (14, 14, 20)
Neck shaping begins on 3rd row of this stripe	D	4
	C	10
	E	2
	B	10
	D	8
	E	18
Joining row is 5th row of this stripe	C	6
	A	4
	B	12 (28, 44, 44)
	D	8 (8, 8, 24)
	E	2
Start underarm shaping on 3rd row of this stripe	C	6
	A	12
	B	4
	D	6
	E	10
	C	2
	B	2
Includes 6 rows Seed St border	A	10

- **This garment is** *knit in one piece,* **beginning at sleeve edge. Always sl the first st of every row purlwise to create a smooth selvedge.**

- **We recommend** *weaving in ends as each color is joined* **whenever possible, to save on finishing time at the end of the piece. However, be mindful that fiber of lighter color will show the woven ends more readily than darker colors. If the woven ends are becoming more visible than desired on RS of work, simply wait until finishing to weave them in.**

- **The yarn is held double** *throughout.* **We recommend winding each skein double stranded. One method suggested: place the open skein around a chair. Snip off ties. Holding both ends of the skein in your hand, wrap the skein into a ball by pulling from both ends simultaneously (one will move to the right, one will move to the left, but both will come together if you wrap slowly and patiently), and you will create one double-stranded ball of yarn.**

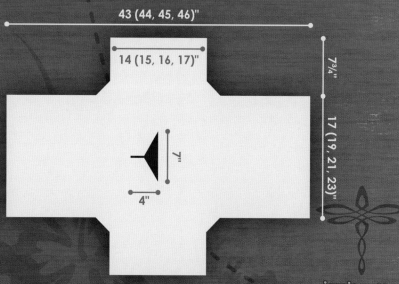

43 (44, 45, 46)"

14 (15, 16, 17)"

7¾"

17 (19, 21, 23)"

7"

4"

jamie murray

Directions

Beg at left sleeve, holding two strands of Color A together, CO 69 (75, 79, 85) sts. Work 6 rows in Seed St, always slipping the first st of every row purlwise for selvedge. Work even in St st for 34 rows, following Stripe Sequence chart.

Shape Underarm: *Inc row (RS):* Sl 1, kfb, k to last 2 sts, kfb, k1.

Next row (WS): Purl.

Repeat these two rows 6 more times - 83, (89, 93, 99) sts.

Shape Sides: At beg of each of next 2 rows CO 66 sts - 215 (221, 225, 231) sts. Work even in St st, following Stripe Sequence chart, until you reach the stripe designated as the beg of neck shaping. Remember to slip the first st of each row purlwise for a smooth selvedge edge.

Divide for Back Neck: *Next row (RS):* Work 107 (110, 112, 115) sts. Place rem sts on second needle for holding.

Work even for 50 rows, following Stripe Sequence chart and continuing to slip first st of each row for selvedge.

Front Neck: Rejoin yarn to held sts at front neck edge. BO 1 st, then work rem 107 (110, 112, 115) sts. Remember, you will need to "back up" on the Stripe Sequence chart to the same place where you began the back neck shaping and match front stripes to the back. Work 2 rows in St st.

Decrease row (RS): *Sl 1, k2tog, k to end.

Next row: Sl 1, purl to end.

Repeat these two rows 9 times more - 97 (100, 102 105) sts remain. Work 2 rows even.

Neck Key: *Next row (RS):* BO 12 sts at neck edge.

Next row (WS): Purl to end, CO 12 sts.

Work 2 rows even.

At neck edge, inc 1 st (kfb) every other row 10 times - 107 (110, 112, 115) sts. Work 2 rows even.

Joining Row (RS): Work across first needle, inc 1 st, work across second needle, consolidating all sts on one needle - 215 (221, 225, 231) sts. Work even following Stripe Sequence chart, until you reach the stripe designated as the beg of underarm shaping.

Shape Sides: At beg of each of next 2 rows BO 66 sts - 83 (89, 93, 99) sts remain.

Inc Row (RS): Sl 1, k2tog, work to last 3 sts, k2tog, k1.

Next Row (WS): Purl.

Repeat these two rows 6 times more - 69 (75, 79, 85) sts. Work even for 34 rows, following Stripe Sequence chart and maintaining selvedge edge, to match first sleeve. Work 6 rows in Seed St. BO loosely.

FINISHING

Weave in all ends. Sew underarm & sleeve seams with tapestry needle. With crochet hook, work 1 round single crochet around neck and bottom openings. Finish with cool iron (set on "silk" or similar low setting) on wrong side of work only. Silken Straw softens both with knitting and with pressing of the fiber. *Do not drag the iron;* rather, lift and place it over entire work, smoothing seams and relaxing the fiber.

the *Muse*

by M. Diane Brown

Oh, the ephemeral nature of the Muse!

She comes, she goes, but she changes you
with every passing state of grace.
Calliope, Clio, Erato, Euterpe, Melpomene,
Polyhymnia, Terpsichore, Thalia, and Urania
— the Nine Greek Muses presided over the
arts and the sciences. May they long continue
to inspire poets, painters, sculptors, musicians,
philosophers, and most especially, knitters!

Beauty and inspiration synthesize in this
ethereal and wonderfully wearable design.
Knit from soft and sensual Haiku, the delicate
lace pattern and scalloped edge are feminine
and flattering. May the subtleties of this classic
cardigan incite your creative muse.

finished size

Chest: 32 (36, 40, 44)"
Length: 22 (23, 23, 24)"
Sleeve length: 24 (25, 25, 26)"

materials

5 (5, 6, 6) skeins
Alchemy Yarns Haiku
Shown in 41f – Vermillion

US size 6 (4 mm) straight
or 24" circular needles
(or size needed to obtain gauge)

US size 5 (3.75 mm) straight
or 24" circular needles

US size 3 (3.25 mm)
24" circular needles

Tapestry needle

Stitch holders

Stitch markers

gauge

22 sts and 28 rows = 4"
in lace pattern (see chart),
using larger needles

Seed Stitch

(worked over an odd number of sts):
Row 1 (RS): *K1, p1,
repeat from * to last st, end k1.
Repeat this row for pattern.

Directions

BACK

With US size 5 (3.75 mm) needles and *double* strand of yarn, CO 89 (97, 109, 117) sts. Work in Seed St for 2 rows, ending with RS facing for the next row. Change to US size 6 (4 mm) needles.

Set-up row: Work 3 (7, 3, 7) sts in Seed St, pm, work first row of lace chart 4 (4, 5, 5) times on next 40 (40, 50, 50) sts, pm, work 3 (3, 3, 3) sts in Seed St, pm, work first row of lace chart 4 (4, 5, 5) times over 40 (40, 50, 50) sts, pm, work last 3 (7, 3, 7) sts in Seed St.

Cont in Seed St and lace pattern as established until work measures 2 (2, 3, 3)" from cast-on edge, ending with RS facing for the next row.

Shape waist: Dec 1 st at beg and end of next row and every following 8th row 3 (3, 3, 4) more times - 81 (89, 101, 107) sts rem. Work 1" without shaping, ending with RS facing for the next row. Inc 1 st at beg and end of next row and every following 8th row until you are back to original st count - 89 (97, 109, 117) sts.

Work without further shaping until back measures 13½" (14, 14, 14½)" from CO edge, ending with RS facing for the next row.

Shape Armholes: BO 3 (3, 4, 5) sts at beg of next 2 rows. Dec 1 st at beg and end of next 4 (4, 5, 5) rows, then dec 1 st at beg and end of every RS row 4 (5, 5, 5) times - 67 (73, 81, 87) sts rem. Cont without shaping until armhole measures 8 (8¼, 8¾, 9)", ending with RS facing for next row.

Shape Shoulders and Back: Work 24 (26, 28, 30) sts in pattern, BO center 19 (21, 25, 27) sts, and work to end of row. Working left shoulder only, work 1 WS row. BO 2 (2, 2, 2) sts at neck edge, work to end of row. Place rem 22 (24, 26, 28) sts on holder. Reattach yarn to right shoulder at neck edge.

BO 2 (2, 2, 2) sts at neck edge, work to end of row. Work final RS row. Place rem 22 (24, 26, 28) sts on holder.

LEFT FRONT

With US size 5 (3.75 mm) needles and *double* strand of yarn, CO 23 (25, 29, 33) sts. Work 2 rows in Seed St. Change to US size 6 (4 mm) needle and proceed as follows: Work 3 (7, 3, 7) sts in Seed St, pm, work first row of lace pattern chart over next 20 (18, 26, 26) sts. Work 1 WS row.

Shape center front and waist: *Next row (Inc row):* Work in pattern to last st, m1, k1. Repeat inc row every RS row 10 (13, 13, 14) more times; then every 4th row 8 (8, 9, 9) times, making sure to incorporate new sts into existing lace pattern. **AT THE SAME TIME** work waist shaping at beg of RS rows to match back. When waist shaping and center front increases are complete, you should have 42 (47, 52, 57) sts.

Cont with Seed St and lace pattern until piece measures 11½ (12, 12½, 13)", ending with RS facing for the next row.

Shape front neckline and armholes: *Next row (dec row):* Work in pattern to last 2 sts, K2tog. Repeat dec row on next RS row, then every 4th row 2 (2, 2, 5) times, then every 6th row 5 (7, 8, 7) times. **AT THE SAME TIME** when work measures 13½ (14, 14, 14½)", BO 3 (3, 4, 5) sts at beg of RS row, then dec 1 st at armhole edge every row 4 (4, 5, 5) times, then every RS row 4 (5, 5, 5) times. Cont until armhole measures same as back - 22 (24, 26, 28) sts rem. Place shoulder sts on holder.

RIGHT FRONT

With US size 5 (3.75 mm) needles and *double* strand of yarn, CO 23 (25, 29, 33) sts. Work 2 rows in Seed St. Change to US size 6 (4 mm) needle and proceed as follows: work first row of lace pattern chart over 20 (18, 26, 26) sts, pm, work rem 3 (7, 3, 7) sts in Seed St.

Work 1 WS row.

- **Yarn is worked doubled for the body of the jacket, but it is used singly for the sleeves and the ruffle around sleeve cuffs and body.**

- **To avoid striping and/or pooling of color, use 2 skeins of yarn as you knit, alternating 2 rows from one skein and 2 rows from another.**

- **When increasing and decreasing in lace pattern, work in St st until increases and decreases are matched. This will insure the accuracy of the st count. Work all increases and decreases in pattern when working in Seed St.**

Shape center front and waist: *Next row (Inc row):* K1, m1, work in pattern to end of row. Repeat inc row every RS row 10 (13, 13, 14) more times; then every 4th row 8 (8, 9, 9) times, making sure to incorporate new sts into existing lace pattern. AT THE SAME TIME work waist shaping at end of RS rows to match back. When waist shaping and center front increases are complete, you should have 42 (47, 52, 57) sts.

Cont with Seed St and lace pattern until piece measures 11½ (12, 12½, 13)", ending with RS facing for the next row.

Shape front neckline and armholes: *Next row (dec row):* K2tog, work in pattern to end of row. Repeat dec row on next RS row, then every 4th row 2 (2, 2, 5) times, then every 6th row 5 (7, 8, 7) times. **AT THE SAME TIME**

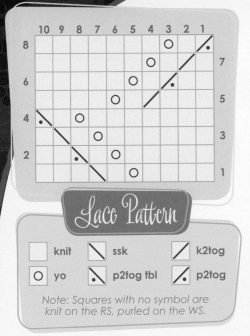

Lace Pattern

☐ knit	◣ ssk	◢ k2tog
◯ yo	◺ p2tog tbl	◿ p2tog

Note: Squares with no symbol are knit on the RS, purled on the WS.

when work measures 13½ (14, 14, 14½)", BO 3 (3, 4, 5) sts at beg of WS row, then dec 1 st at armhole edge every row 4 (4, 5, 5) times, then every RS row 4 (5, 5, 5) times. Cont until armhole measures same as back – 22 (24, 26, 28) sts rem. Place shoulder sts on holder.

SLEEVES

With size 5 (3.75 mm) needles and *single* strand of yarn, CO 57 (61, 65, 67) sts and work 2 rows in seed st, increasing 1 st at the end of last row. Change to size 6 (4 mm) needles.

Set-up row (RS): Work 9 (11, 13, 9) sts in Seed St, pm, work first row of lace chart 4 (4, 4, 5) times over next 40 (40, 40, 50) sts, pm, work last 9 (11, 13, 9) sts in Seed St. Work next 7 rows without shaping, ending with RS facing.

Cuff shaping: *Next row (dec row):* Dec 1 st at beg and end of row. Repeat dec row every 4th row 5 (7, 7, 5) times more. Work in Seed St and lace pattern without shaping for 1", ending with RS facing for next row.

Sleeve increases: *Next row (Inc row):* Work in seed st to marker, m1, sl marker, work to marker, sl marker, m1, work in seed st to end of row. Repeat inc row every RS row 4 (4, 4, 2) times more, then every 4th row 9 (7, 6, 4) times, then every 6th row 4 (8, 8, 10) times - 82 (86, 88, 90) sts. Cont without shaping until sleeve measures 16 (17, 17, 17½)" from cast-on edge, ending with RS facing for next row.

Shape Sleeve Cap: BO 3 (3, 4, 5) sts at beg of next 2 rows. Then dec 1 st at beg and end of every row 5 (5, 6, 6) times. Work 1 (1, 0, 0) row. Dec 1 st at beg and end of every RS row 5 (5, 5, 6) times, then every 4th row 4 (4, 5, 6) times. BO 2 sts at beg of the next 8 (8, 8, 4) rows. BO 5 (3, 3, 4) sts at beg of next 2 (4, 2, 2) rows. BO remaining 22 (24, 26, 28) sts.

FINISHING

Join fronts to back at shoulders using 3-needle bind-off method.

Cuff ruffle: At edge of sleeve, with RS facing, using size 3 circular needle and *single* strand of yarn, pick up and knit 69 (75, 81, 81) sts. Work 3 rows in Seed St, ending with RS facing for next row.

First Inc Row (RS): Kfb in every st.

Second Inc (WS): *K1, kfb, repeat from * to end of row – 207 (225, 243, 243) sts.

BO all sts.

Repeat for other sleeve.

Back ruffle: At bottom edge of back, with RS side facing, size 3 circular needle and *single* strand of yarn, pick up and knit 91 (99, 111, 119) sts. Work 3 rows Seed St and two inc rows as for cuff – 273 (297, 333, 357) sts. BO all sts.

Front ruffle: Beg at lower edge of right front, with RS facing, size 3 circular needle and *single* strand of yarn, pick up and knit 369 (381, 393, 403) sts along right front, back neck, and left front. Work 3 rows Seed St and two inc rows as for cuff – 1107 (1143, 1179, 1209) sts. BO all sts.

Sew sleeves into armholes, evenly distributing any fullness in cap. Sew side and sleeve seams. Block lace very lightly.

Corkscrew ties: With *single* strand of yarn and size 3 needle, CO 50 sts. Knit into front, back and front of each st (making 3 sts out of 1) – 150 sts. BO. Make 2.

Sew ties to right and left front edges at beginning of neck shaping behind ruffle.

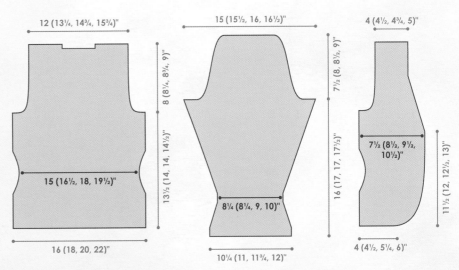

Josephine Baker's Bag

by Gina Wilde

Josephine started her career dancing as a child street performer in St. Louis. Now remembered as a quintessential expatriate—American by birth, French by choice—she became the indisputable star of the Parisian Revue. Known for appearing nearly nude onstage with her diamond-collared cheetah Chiquita, who occasionally jumped into the orchestra pit to terrify the musicians, Josephine was also a devout leader for the Civil Rights Movement. She adopted 12 children of 12 nationalities in her lifetime, which she called her "Rainbow Family." In the words of Ernest Hemingway, Ms. Baker was

"…the most sensational woman anyone ever saw."

If Josephine had been a fiber artist, perhaps she would have created bold color fields of texture on which she could shimmy those fine silk tassels! The nature of our Silken Straw yarn calls for precisely such playful interpretation and expression — bold color, unapologetic shine, and curious texture, to accentuate the positive!

finished size

10" x 10" without handles

materials

Alchemy Yarns Silken Straw, shown in
81f – **House Finch (A)** – 1 skein
71f – **Rich Berry (B)** – 2 skeins
48a – **Passion Flower (C)** – 1 skein

US Size 5 (3.75 mm) needles
(or size needed to obtain gauge)

**US Size 5 (3.75 mm)
double-pointed needles**

US Size F (3.75 mm) crochet hook

Stitch holders

gauge

22 sts = 4" in Woven Stitch
on *US size 5 needles, with 2 strands
of yarn held together*

Woven Stitch

Row 1 (RS): *K1, wyif sl 1,
repeat from * to last st, k1.
Rows 2 and 4: P
Row 3: K2, * wyif sl 1, k1,
repeat from * to last st, k1.
*Repeat rows 1–4 for
Woven Stitch.*

I-cord

Knit all sts, * slide the work to the opposite end of the needle, bring yarn around behind sts, and knit them again from the same direction. Working yarn is pulled from the last st to the first st each time a new row is started. Repeat from * for as many rows as needed.

Directions

BODY OF BAG (MAKE TWO)

With double strand of Color A, CO 55 sts. Work in Woven St for 3½". With Color C, k 4 rows. Do not cut Color C; leave hanging at side of work.

Set-up row for color blocks: With RS facing, and Color B, work in Woven St across 17 sts, while loosely carrying Color C on WS of work; k 3 sts in Color C, carrying Color B behind work; work remaining 35 sts in Color B in Woven St to end of row.

Continue working Color B in Woven St and Color C in Garter St until piece measures approx 10" from beginning.

Make straps (2 per each side of bag): *Next row (RS):* Bind off first 4 sts in Woven St; place next 9 sts on holder; bind off remaining sts in Woven St.

Place first 4 sts from holder onto needle, leaving rem 5 sts on holder. Work I-cord for approx 13", or to desired length. BO. *Note:* The straps are intended to extend beyond the edge of the bag. The outside strap extends approx 1½" below top of bag, and the inside strap approx 2" as shown in photo.

Place 5 sts from holder onto needle. Bind off first st, then work I-cord on next 4 sts for approx 13". BO.

> ### Note
> **Yarn is worked double throughout, except when making tassels.**

Gusset

With smaller needles, CO 12 sts in color B. Work in Garter St as follows:

- Color B for 5½"
- Color C for ½"
- Color A for 15½"
- Color C for ½"
- Color B for 5½"

BO.

FINISHING

Tassels: Cut a piece of heavy card stock 3½" wide by 5" long. Draw two lines the length of the card 1" from the edge, with 1½" between the lines. With Color A, wrap the card neatly with yarn in tight parallel lines from one line to the other. Secure the ends with a piece of tape. Cut a strand of color B about 24" long and thread it through a tapestry needle. Insert the needle under all strands at the top of the card. Pull tightly and knot securely. With a strand of waste yarn, tie other end of tassel in the same way. Slip yarn off card. Cut a strand of color C approx 36" long and thread on a tapestry needle. Wrap the neck of the tassel tightly, beginning about 1" from tied top of tassel and extending for about 1" as shown in photo. Wind smoothly and in one direction only, allowing each strand to lie neatly next to the strand before it. When wrapping is the desired height, pass the needle directly up through the center of the wrapped portion, then down again, and out through the bottom of the tassel. Secure other end of wrap in the same way. Cut loops at the bottom of the tassel, removing scrap yarn. Make a cord for the tassel by crocheting a chain to desired length (approx 3") using the long ends of color B tied at the head of the tassel. Make 2nd tassel to match.

Assembly: Lightly block pieces, with warm iron on WS of work. With Silken Straw, it is okay to use steam, even though it is 100% silk. (This fiber loves a hot iron!)

With wrong sides together, Color C (double stranded) and size F crochet hook, and using single crochet, join gusset to edges of first body piece as follows: beginning at top edge and lining up colors in each piece, work down first side, along bottom of bag, and up to the top of second side. Repeat for other side of bag, joining gusset to 2nd body piece.

Sew straps in place, with outer strap inset approx 1" from left outside edge (to match placement on the right side), extending approx 1½" below top of bag. Inside strap should extend approx 2" below top of bag, and should be inset to match right side. Repeat for other side of bag.

Attach tassels to the ends of I-cord on one side of bag. If desired, make 2 additional tassels, to mirror tassel placement on other side of bag.

Weave in ends. Block lightly to size if needed.

Tie Me Up! Tie Me Down!

Desire, passion, family and identity characterize the films of Pedro Almodóvar. Often outrageous, his movies are a journey to lands of unbridled imagination, alive with characters and situations that are deep and complex. Almodóvar weaves unforgettable tales of truth, beauty, and despair.

This clever unisex tie stars our wildly unique Silken Straw fiber, a yarn that displays amazing stitch definition while exhibiting qualities of extraordinary strength. The mighty miter in the center provides both textural interest and clever construction, inspired by the legendary Spanish filmmaker.

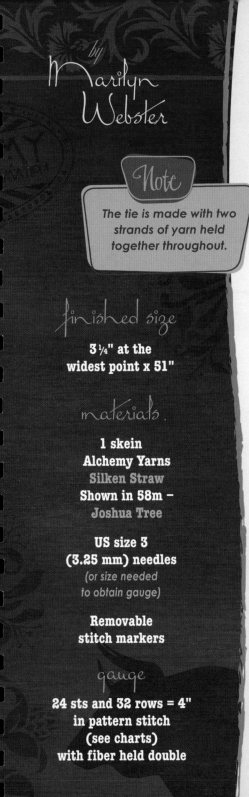

by
Marilyn Webster

Note

The tie is made with two strands of yarn held together throughout.

finished size

3¼" at the widest point x 51"

materials

**1 skein
Alchemy Yarns**
Silken Straw
Shown in 58m –
Joshua Tree

**US size 3
(3.25 mm) needles**
*(or size needed
to obtain gauge)*

**Removable
stitch markers**

gauge

**24 sts and 32 rows = 4"
in pattern stitch
(see charts)
with fiber held double**

Directions

With two strands of yarn held together, CO 29 sts.

Work from charts as follows:

Work rows 1–5 of **Chart A**, then repeat rows 2–5 until piece measures 2¾" along side edge.

Work rows 6–7 of chart A (27 sts).

Repeat rows 8–11 of chart A until pieces measures 5½" along side edge.

Work rows 12–13 of chart A (25 sts).

Repeat rows 14–17 of chart A until piece measures 8¼" along side edge.

Work rows 18–19 of chart A (23 sts).

Change to **Chart B.** Repeat rows 1–4 of chart B until piece measures 11" along side edge.

Work rows 5–6 of chart B (21 sts).

Repeat rows 7–10 of chart B until piece measures 13¾" along side edge.

Work rows 11–12 of chart B (19 sts).

Repeat rows 13–16 of chart B until piece measures 16½" along side edge.

Work rows 17–18 of chart B (17 sts).

Repeat rows 19–22 until piece measures 19¼" along side edge.

Change to **Chart C.** Work rows 1–2 (15 sts).

Repeat rows 3–6 of chart C until piece measures 22" along side edge.

Work rows 7–8 of chart C (13 sts).

Repeat rows 9–12 of chart C until piece measures 24¾" along side edge.

Work rows 13–14 of chart C (11 sts.)

Repeat rows 15–18 of chart C until piece measures 27½" along side edge.

Work rows 19–20 of chart C (9 sts). Place a marker on this final decrease row.

Repeat rows 21–24 of chart C until 13" past marker (Piece will measure 40½").

Change to **Chart D.** Work rows 1–2 of chart D (11 sts).

Repeat rows 3–6 of chart D for 4" (Piece will measure 44½").

Work rows 7–8 of chart D (13 sts).

Repeat rows 9–12 of chart D for 4½". (Piece will measure 49").

Work rows 13–22 of chart D (3 sts).

Work a double decrease and pull fiber through to bind off.

FINISHING

Weave in ends. Block lightly by holding a steam iron above the tie. To avoid flattening the texture, do not actually touch the tie with the iron.

Chart A

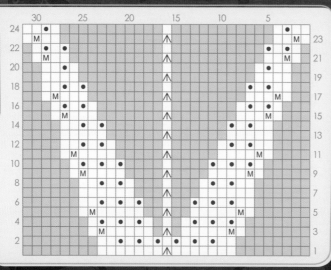

Chart B

Chart C

Chart D

Legend:

- ▨ No Stitch
- ☐ **Knit:** *RS:* K / *WS:* P
- ⊡ **Purl:** *RS:* P / *WS:* K
- **M** **Make One**
  - *RS:* Lift strand in between st just worked and the next st, K into back of this thread.
  - *WS:* Lift strand in between st just worked and the next st, P into back of this thread.
- ⋀ **Central Double Dec**
  - *RS:* Sl 1st and 2nd st tog as if to K. K 1 st. Pass 2 slipped sts over the K st.

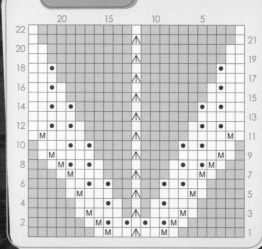

Silken Straw

A sport weight
pure silk floss with
a unique texture.
Lovely worked double
stranded if the small gauge
scares you. This fiber
reaches its full soft
and drapey potential
when introduced
to a hot iron.

100% Silk

2 FINE

Approx 236 yards **(215 m)**
in a 40 gram **skein**

Recommended gauge:
24 sts = 4" on US size 4 needles

*To see the full range of glorious colors
available in Silken Straw, please visit our
website at* **www.alchemyyarns.com**

the Origamist

by Sandi Rosner & Gina Wilde

Practiced since the Edo Period of the 1600s, the exquisite art of paper folding is a significant part of Japanese culture. Origami butterflies were made to represent the bride and groom at Shinto wedding ceremonies. Samurai warriors exchanged gifts adorned with noshi, a good luck totem made of folded sheets of paper.

The Origamist, in Silk Purse, is a creative exercise in geometry and patterning, culminating in a graceful cardigan. Artistically unparalleled, this piece folds into myriad interesting shapes—wear it long with elegant drape, wrap both ends behind the back, or throw one (or both) lengths over the shoulder. The possibilities are all luxurious, with each configuration finding you wrapped in a lush textural experience.

finished size

Chest: 36 (40, 44, 48)"
Length: 16 (17, 18, 19)"

materials

**9 (10, 11, 12) skeins
Alchemy Yarns Silk Purse
Shown in 42m – Silver**

US size 6 (4 mm) needles
(or size needed to obtain gauge)

Size H (5 mm) crochet hook

Stitch holders

gauge

**21 sts and 28 rows = 4"
after steam blocking
in Twin Rib Stitch**

Twin Rib Stitch

**Row 1 (RS): * K3, P3,
repeat from * to end of row
Row 2 (WS): * K1, P1,
repeat from * to end of row**
Repeat these two rows for pattern.

16 (16, 18, 18)

16 (17, 18, 19)"

8 (8½, 9, 9½)"

8 (8½, 9, 9½)"

18 (20, 22, 24)"

29 (27½, 30, 29)"

4"

16 (17, 18, 19)"

8 (9, 10½, 11½)"

Directions

BACK

CO 96 (108, 114, 126) sts. Work in Twin Rib Stitch until piece measures 8 (8½, 9, 9½)" from beginning.

Shape armholes: Maintaining pattern as established, BO 3 (5, 5, 7) sts at beg of next 2 rows, then dec 1 st at beg and end of every RS row 2 (6, 5, 9) times - 86 (86, 94, 94) sts. Cont without shaping until piece measures 16 (17, 18, 19)" from beg.

Work 24 (24, 26, 26) sts in pattern and place these sts on a holder. BO next 38 (38, 42, 42) sts for back neck. Work rem 24 (24, 26, 26) sts and place on another holder.

RIGHT FRONT

CO 42 (48, 54, 60) sts. Work 2 rows in Twin Rib Stitch. Cont in pattern, use Cable cast on method to CO 2 sts at beg of every RS row 58 (54, 57, 54) times and **AT THE SAME TIME**, when same length as back to armholes, BO 3 (5, 5, 7) sts at beg of next WS row, then dec 1 st at end of every RS row 2 (6, 5, 9) times - 153 (145, 158, 152) sts.

Cont without shaping until same length as back to shoulders.

Next row (RS): Work 129 (121, 132, 126) sts in pattern and place on a holder. Work rem 24 (24, 26, 26) sts and place on another holder for shoulder.

LEFT FRONT

CO 42 (48, 54, 60) sts. Work 3 rows in Twin Rib Stitch. Cont in pattern, use Cable cast on method to CO 2 sts at beg of every WS row 58 (54, 57, 54) times and **AT THE SAME TIME**, when same length as back to armholes, BO 3 (5, 5, 7) sts at beg

of next RS row, then dec 1 st at beg of every RS row 2 (6, 5, 9) times - 153 (145, 158, 152) sts.

Cont without shaping until same length as back to shoulders.

Next row (RS): Work 24 (24, 26, 26) sts in pattern and place on a holder for shoulder. Work rem 129 (121, 132, 126) sts and place on another holder.

Join fronts to back at shoulders using 3-needle BO.

COLLAR

Replace sts from right front holder on needle and work in pattern as established. Pick up and knit 41 (41, 44, 44) sts along back neck. Place sts from left front holder on needle and work in pattern as established - 299 (283, 308, 296) sts. Work in pattern as established for 4". BO loosely.

SLEEVES

CO 3 sts. Work 1 row Twin Rib Stitch. Maintaining pattern, use Cable cast on method to CO 2 sts at beg of every row until 39 (39, 43, 43) sts on needle. Cont in pattern, inc 1 st at beg and end of every 10th row 10 (11, 11, 12) times - 59 (61, 65, 67) sts. Cont without shaping until piece measures 19½ (20, 20, 20½)" from point (see note above for tip on measuring).

BO 3 (5, 5, 7) sts at beg of next 2 rows, then dec 1 st at beg and end of every RS row 3 (6, 5, 9) times, then dec 1 st at beg and end of every 4th row 9 (5, 7, 3) times - 29 (29, 31, 29) sts.

BO 2 sts at beg of next 2 rows. BO rem 25 (25, 27, 25) sts.

Note

This stitch pattern in combination with this yarn produces a fabric that will tend to expand both vertically and horizontally when blocked. Do not be alarmed if the pieces look narrow while you are knitting them. The only place this may cause you problems is in the sleeve length. You will need to be careful to block as you go while you are knitting the sleeves so they don't end up too long. When you are three to four inches short of the desired length for your sleeve, move the knitting to the cable of your circular needle, take it to your ironing board, and steam the knitting. Do not allow the iron to touch the fabric; just give it lots of steam. Smooth out the knitting, stretching it in all directions, and let it cool. Now measure. Continue to knit a little, steam again, and measure until the sleeve is the desired length to the underarm.

FINISHING

Sew sleeves into armholes. Sew side and sleeve seams. Steam block as indicated in note.

Work 1 round of single crochet around lower edge of sleeves and around diagonal and lower edges of body. Steam block again.

Slanted Eyelet Scarf

If Paris is the City of Love,
then Florence must be the City of Passion.
In this mecca of extraordinary history, no
visit is complete without a stroll through the
dazzling Uffizi, the awe-inspiring experience of
Brunelleschi's Dome, and a walk through Boboli
Gardens at sunset. A destination that ensures a
celebration of the senses, Firenze embraces
all that is lovely and beautiful.

In honor of such cultural riches, this scarf is
a wonderfully worthy knit. Only one skein of
yarn is needed to work the simple two-row lace
repeat. Designed to engage the beginning or
experienced lace knitter, the end result is a
flowing, elegant, and very wearable accessory.
Readily adaptable to any of Alchemy's
fiber offerings, we show it in Silken Straw.

by Sandi Rosner

finished size

Approx 4" x 50" after blocking

materials

**1 skein
Alchemy Yarns Silken Straw
Shown in 59c – Rainforest**

US size 4 (3.5 mm) needles
(or size needed to obtain gauge)

• • • or • • •

**1 skein
Alchemy Yarns Silk Purse**

US size 6 (4.25 mm) needles
(or size needed to obtain gauge)

gauge

24 sts = 4" in Eyelet Pattern
in either Silk Purse or Silken Straw

Eyelet Pattern

Row 1: K 4, * YO, K 3, k2tog,
repeat from * 3 times more,
YO, k2tog, K 3
Row 2: K 3, P 23, K 3

Directions

Loosely CO 34 sts
for Silken Straw, or
29 sts for Silk Purse.

K 4 rows for Garter
st border. Change
to eyelet pattern
and work until
approx 4 yards of
yarn remain. K 4
rows for border.

BO loosely.

FINISHING

Weave in ends.
Block your scarf
by hand washing
gently in warm
water. Lay the
damp scarf out on
a flat surface and
stretch it to the
desired finished
measurements.
Stretching will
open up the
eyelet pattern.
Straighten the
edges, and allow
the scarf to dry
undisturbed.
When your scarf is
completely dry, it
will be wonderfully
drapey and open.

Femme Fatale
by Gina Wilde

That voodoo that you do...

Held at one border by the mighty Mississippi River and on all sides by a proud heritage, New Orleans is a Queen of a City. Home to the legendary Blues and underground music scenes (think Jazz Fest, Tipitina's, and Preservation Hall), as well as Cajun cooking and Old South charm (including the seedier side of strip clubs and voodoo shops), New Orleans is unique among American cities. Though she may get battered and bruised, *the beautiful Lady always stands proud.*

In this Streetcar Named Desire of a sweater, the ephemeral Haiku fiber is barely there, soft as a whisper, elegant and sensual. The uncomplicated pullover, quick as a flash to knit, is designed to be worn over a sexy camisole. Femme Fatale brings new meaning to "light as a feather" fiber. The bell sleeves give the sense of flattering femininity, and will leave you casting the best of spells when you wear this timeless design.

finished size

Chest: 36 (40, 44, 48)"

materials

3 (4, 5, 6) skeins
Alchemy Yarns Haiku
Shown in 100c – Azalea Trail

1 (1, 1, 1) skein
Alchemy Yarns Silk Purse
Shown in 100c – Azalea Trail

US size 10 (6 mm) needles
(or size needed to obtain gauge)

Size E crochet hook

Tapestry needle

Stitch holders

gauge

18 sts and 24 rows = 4"
in Garter Stitch

Directions

BACK

Using **Haiku**, CO 81 (91, 99, 109) sts. Work in Garter St for 13 (13½, 14, 15)", or desired length to underarm.

Armhole Shaping: At beg of next 2 rows, bind off 5 (5, 5, 5) sts. At beg of following 2 rows, bind off 3 (3, 3, 3) sts. At beg of following 2 rows, BO 0 (0, 3, 3) sts. Dec 1 st at beg and end of every RS row 1 (4, 4, 7) times - 63 (67, 69, 73) sts.

Cont to work in Garter St until armhole measures 9 (9½, 9½, 10)". Place sts on holder.

FRONT

Work same as for back until armhole measures 6 (6½, 6½, 7)".

Neck shaping: K 24 (25, 25, 26) sts, join 2nd ball of yarn and loosely bind off center 15 (17, 19, 21) sts, K rem sts. Working both sides at once, dec 1 st at neck edge every RS row 7 (7, 7, 7) times – 17 (18, 18 19) sts rem on each side. Work even until same length as back to shoulders. Place sts on holders.

SLEEVES

Note: Sleeves are worked from the top down.

Using **Haiku**, CO 72 (70, 70, 68) sts. Working in Garter St, inc 1 st at beg and end of every RS row 1 (4, 4, 7) times. CO 0 (0, 3, 3) sts

at beg of next 2 rows, then CO 3 (3, 3, 3) sts at beg of following 2 rows, then CO 5 (5, 5, 5) sts at beg of following 2 rows – 90 (94, 100, 104) sts. Cont in Garter St, dec 1 st at beg and end of every 6th row 6 (0, 0, 0) times, then every 4th row 14 (23, 25, 26) times – 46 (48, 50, 52) sts. Work even until piece measures 18 (18, 18½ 19)".

Bell shaping: Cont in Garter St, inc 7 sts evenly spaced across next row. Repeat this increase every 8 rows 2 times more. 67 (69, 71, 73) sts. Work 3 more rows in Garter St. Bind off loosely.

FINISHING

Lightly block pieces with warm iron on wrong side of work (use pressing cloth) if necessary.

Join front to back at shoulders using three needle bind off.

Sew sleeves to armholes, easing in any fullness at shoulder. Sew side and sleeve seams.

Borders: With RS facing and **Silk Purse**, work 1 row single crochet around bottom edge. Work 1 round picot as follows: *Work 1 sc in each of next 2 sts, chain 3, join with a slip st to top of last sc; repeat from * around edge. Fasten off. Repeat for neck and sleeve borders.

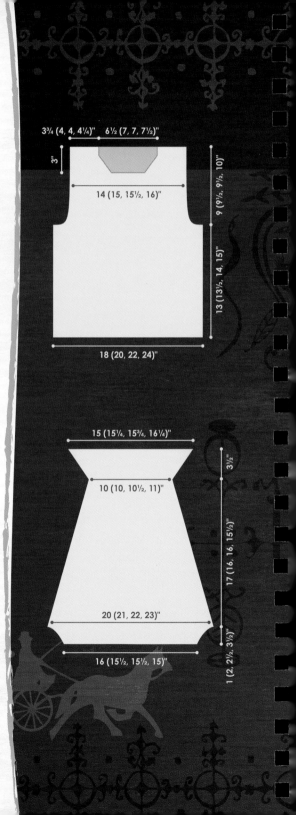

Haiku

A fine gauge blend of silk and mohair,
best worked on a larger needle than you
might think, so the mohair can bloom.
The perfect medium
for a knitted lace masterpiece,
this yarn is also a great team player,
contributing its soft halo
when blended with Silk Purse.

3 LIGHT

40% Silk / **60%** Mohair
Approx **325** yards (**295 m**)
in a **25 gram skein**
Recommended gauge:
20 sts = 4" on US size 7 needles

To see the full range of luscious colors
available in Haiku, please visit our
website at **www.alchemyyarns.com**

Cable Cardigan

by Gina Wilde

From the ghosts of the Beat poets in North Beach to the good hippies of Haight Street and all points in between, San Francisco has made a living opening its collective arms to free spirits everywhere. The Summer of Love still lives in this Golden Gate city, where hearts are routinely left high on a hill, and dreams still come true. The Bay Area is a place where diversity is celebrated and the Wild West still exists in a modern landscape.

Sensuous silk is knit in a simply styled cardigan, embellished with a tidy cable along the seed stitch front borders. Timeless in design, with a nod to the classic eras that have gone before, this piece is destined to become an absolute favorite, to knit and to wear.

finished size

Chest: 34 (36, 38, 40, 42, 44)"

materials

7 (7, 8, 9, 9, 10) skeins
Alchemy Yarns Silk Purse
Shown in 98c – Mediterranean

US size 4 (3.5 mm)
and 5 (3.75 mm) needles
(or size needed to obtain gauge)

Tapestry needle

6 buttons, 5/8"

gauge

22 sts and 28 rows = 4"
in St st, using larger needles

Seed Stitch

(work on odd number of sts)
All rows: *K1, p1, repeat
from * last st, k1.

Cable Pattern

Row 1, 3 and 5: K
Row 2, 4 and 6: P
Row 7: C6B on Left Front,
or C6F on Right Front.
Row 8: Repeat row 2.

5 (5½, 5½, 6, 6½, 6¾)"

2"

6½ (7, 7½, 8, 8, 8½)"

12"

17 (18, 19, 20, 21, 22)"

1"

8½ (9, 9½, 10, 10, 10½)"

13¼ (13¾, 14¾, 15½, 16, 16½)"

12"

10¼ (10¾, 11½, 12, 12½, 13)"

Directions

BACK

With smaller needles, CO 93 (99, 105, 111, 115, 121) sts. Work in Seed stitch for 1". Change to larger needles and cont in St st until back measures 12" or desired length to underarm.

Shape Armholes: BO 3 (3, 4, 4, 5, 5) sts at beg of next 2 rows.

Row 1: K2, SSK, k to last 4 sts, k2tog, k2.

Row 2: Purl.

Repeat rows 1 & 2 a total of 30 (31, 33, 35, 35, 37) times. Place rem 27 (31, 31, 33, 35, 37) sts on holder.

LEFT FRONT

With smaller needles, CO 57 (59, 61, 63, 67, 69) sts. Work in Seed st for 1". Change to larger needles.

Row 1: Cont in St st to last 19 sts, Seed st 2 sts, k6, Seed st 2 sts, k2, Seed st 7 sts (front band).

Row 2: Seed st 7 sts, p2, Seed st 2, p6, Seed st 2 sts, purl to end of row.

Repeat these two rows working cable pattern as detailed above on the 6 sts between the Seed st panels until front measures 12", or same as for back.

Shape armhole: BO 3 (3, 4, 4, 5, 5) sts at armhole edge. Dec 1 st at armhole edge as for back 23 (24, 26, 28, 28, 30) times. 31, (32, 31, 30, 34, 34) sts remain.

Shape neck: Work sts of front Seed st band and place these 7 sts on a holder. Work to end of row. Cont to dec 1 st at armhole edge 7 times more and **AT THE SAME TIME** BO 4 (4, 4, 4, 4, 4) sts at neck edge once and 2 sts at neck edge every other row 6 times. Place rem 1 (2, 1, 0, 4, 4) sts on holder.

RIGHT FRONT

Work as for left front, reversing cable pattern (work C6F instead of C6B) and all shaping, and incorporating buttonholes as follows. First buttonhole should be worked approx ½" from bottom edge.

Buttonhole row: At front edge Seed st 2 sts, BO 2 sts, Seed st 2 sts, work to end of row.

Next row: CO 2 sts directly above those bound off on previous row.

Make 4 more buttonholes evenly spaced, with final buttonhole worked approx 2" before beg of neck shaping. The 6th buttonhole will be worked in neck band.

SLEEVES

Note: Sleeves are intended to be three quarters length.

With smaller needles, CO 57 (59, 63, 67, 69, 71) sts. Work in Seed st for 1". Change to larger needles and cont in St st, inc 1 st at beg and end of every 6th row 8 (8, 9, 9, 9, 10) times. Work even on 73 (75, 81, 85, 87, 91) sts until sleeve measures 12" from beg.

Shape raglan cap: BO 3 (3, 4, 4, 5, 5) sts at beginning of next 2 rows. Dec 1 st each end every other row in same manner as for back 30 (31, 33, 35, 35, 37) times. Place rem 7 sts on holder.

FINISHING

Lightly block pieces with warm iron on wrong side of work (use pressing cloth).

Sew sleeves to front and back armholes. Sew side and sleeve seams.

Neckband: With smaller needles, pick up and knit 93 (95, 97, 99, 101, 103) sts around edge, including sts from holders. *Note:* This number is not meant to be set in stone; rather, it is a suggestion, and we hope you will work intuitively, picking up sts evenly where necessary, while incorporating all sts from the holders. The total should be an odd number of sts. Work Seed st for 3 rows. Make buttonhole at beg of 4th row. Cont in Seed st until band measures 1". Loosely BO all sts.

Weave in ends. Block lightly to size. Attach buttons opposite buttonholes.

the *Ingénue*

by Lauren Lax

The dream of being discovered at the soda shop, or at Starbucks. Avoiding the casting couch, or the freeways at rush hour. Being ready for the close-up, or at least willing to work as a stand-in. For nearly a century, a youthfully exuberant parade of Hollywood hopefuls have bought that one-way ticket to the City of Angels. Part boulevard of broken dreams, part land of opportunity, L.A. makes its indelible impression through films, television and tabloids. The land of palm trees and celebrity has a lasting appeal—despite our better sense of the ways things must really be out there.

Seductive silk and soft feminine lace

take center stage in this remarkably versatile Silk Purse top. Elegant yet playful, clever yet subdued, this is the knit parallel to the new girl in town—the one you know is going to be around for the long run.

finished size

Bust: 30 (32, 34, 36, 38)"

materials

**3 (4, 4, 5, 5) skeins
Alchemy Yarns Silk Purse
Shown in 91m – Copper**

**US size 6 (4 mm) 24"
circular needles**
(or size needed to obtain gauge)

gauge

22 sts and 28 rows = 4" in St st

Note

This piece starts with the cross-hatch band under the bust. Stitches are picked up from the band and worked down for bottom. Finally stitches are picked up from the other edge of the band and worked up for the bodice.

15 (16, 17, 18, 19)"

7½ (7½, 8, 8¼)"

14 (15, 16, 17, 18)"

2½"

7 (7, 8, 8)"

16.(17, 18, 19, 20)"

3"

2¼ (2½, 2¾, 3, 3¼)"

2 (2, 2½, 2½, 3)"

Directions

CROSS-HATCH BAND

CO 16 sts.

Row 1 (RS): K2, *sl 1, k 1, psso but before dropping the slipped stitch from the left needle, knit into the back of it, repeat from * to last 2 sts, k 2.

Row 2 (WS): P 1, *p2tog, do not slip stitches off the needle, purl the first stitch again, slip both stitches off needle, repeat from * to last st, p 1.

Repeat Rows 1 and 2 until piece measures 28 (30, 32, 34, 36)". BO all sts. Sew cast on and bound off edges together.

BOTTOM (BELOW THE BAND)

With RS facing, pick up and knit 154 (164,176, 188, 200) sts evenly around one edge of band. Join, placing a marker at beg of round and after 77 (82, 88, 94, 100) sts. Cont in St st (k every round) for 3". Inc 1 st before and after each marker on next and every following 7th round 4 (4, 4, 5, 5) more times. Work should measure approx 7 (7, 8, 8, 8)" excluding band. K to marker denoting beg of round. Now you will begin working back and forth in St st on sts between markers for front - 87 (92, 98, 106, 112) sts. The first row will be a purl row.

Front: BO 1 st at beginning of next 10 (10, 12, 12, 14) rows. BO 2 sts at beginning of next 2 rows. BO 4 sts at beginning of next 2 rows. BO remaining 65 (70, 74, 82, 86) sts.

Back: Reattach yarn to sts not yet worked. Repeat as for Front.

BODICE (ABOVE THE BAND)

With RS of cross-hatch band facing, pick up and knit 164 (176, 188, 200, 212) sts evenly around the other edge of band. Join, placing marker at beg of round and after 82 (88, 94, 100, 106) sts. Work in St st for 1". Inc 1 st before and after each marker on next round. Work 6 rounds even. Repeat inc row—172 (184, 196, 208, 220) sts. Work even in St st until bodice measures 2¼ (2½, 2¾, 3, 3¼)" above band. K to marker denoting beg of round. Now you will begin working back and forth in St st on sts between markers—86 (92, 98, 104, 110) sts.

Upper back: BO 6 (7, 8, 8, 9) sts, K to end of row, turn. BO 6 (7, 8, 8, 9) sts, P to end of row. Dec 1 st each at beg and end of every RS row 4 (4, 4, 5, 5) times. When work above armholes measures 3", BO center 14 (14, 16, 16, 18) sts. Working each side separately, dec one stitch on neck edge every right side row 13 (14, 15, 16, 17) times. Work even on 13 (14, 14, 15, 15) sts until armhole measures 7½ (7½, 7¾, 8, 8¼)". BO all sts

Upper Left Front: Reattach yarn to sts left unworked. BO 6 (7, 8, 8, 9) sts. K 37 (39, 41, 44, 46) sts. Place remaining 43 (46, 49, 52, 55) sts on holder. P1 WS row. Dec 1 st each armhole edge every RS row 4 (4, 4, 5, 5) times.

AT THE SAME TIME, at neck edge BO 1 st 3 (3, 3, 4, 3) times, 2 sts 2 (2, 2, 2, 2) times, 4 sts 2 (2, 2, 2, 3) times, 2 sts 1 (1, 2, 2, 2) times, 1 st 3 (4, 4, 4, 3) times. Work even on 13 (14, 14, 15, 15) sts until armhole measures 7½ (7½, 7¾, 8, 8¼)". BO all sts.

Upper Right Front: Rejoin yarn to sts left unworked at *armhole* edge. BO 6 (7, 8, 8, 9) sts, purl to end. Dec 1 st each armhole edge every RS row 4 (4, 4, 5, 5) times. **AT THE SAME TIME,** at neck edge BO 1 st 3 (3, 3, 4, 3) times, 2 sts 2 (2, 2, 2, 2) times, 4 sts 2 (2, 2, 2, 3) times, 2 sts 1 (1, 2, 2, 2) times, 1 st 3 (4, 4, 4, 3) times. Work even on 13 (14, 14, 15, 15) sts until armhole measures 7½ (7½, 7¾, 8, 8¼)". BO all sts.

FINISHING

Sew back to front at shoulders.

Neck edging: Work 1 round sc around neck. Next round: Ch 1, *work 1 sc in each of next 2 sts, ch 3 and join with a slip st to top of last sc; repeat from * around neck, join with slip st to top of beginning ch. Fasten off.

Armhole edging: Work as for neck edging.

Bottom edging: Work as for neck edging.

Weave in ends. Block gently to size.

Math Geek Scarf

Forgoing the maddening crowd of the cafeteria, these girls prefer to take refuge in the quiet confines of the math classroom. No counting calories here—they're shredding square roots and musing on fractals. Space and time converge for 28 minutes of solace.

Don't be intimidated by the name— even those with less than geeky math skills will thrill to the unusual mitered construction and the delightful form rendered by the classic short row design. We feature the piece in Silk Purse and Silken Straw, though it will adapt to many other fibers, as the piece is not gauge-specific.

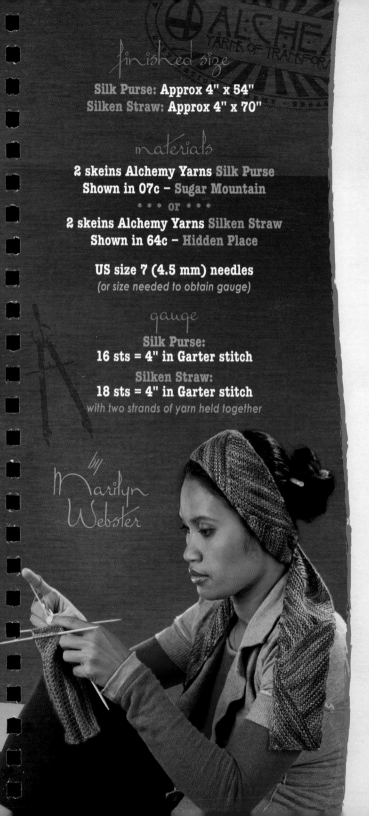

finished size

Silk Purse: Approx 4" x 54"
Silken Straw: Approx 4" x 70"

materials

2 skeins Alchemy Yarns Silk Purse
Shown in 07c – Sugar Mountain
• • • or • • •
2 skeins Alchemy Yarns Silken Straw
Shown in 64c – Hidden Place

US size 7 (4.5 mm) needles
(or size needed to obtain gauge)

gauge

Silk Purse:
16 sts = 4" in Garter stitch
Silken Straw:
18 sts = 4" in Garter stitch
with two strands of yarn held together

by
Marilyn Webster

Directions

TRIANGLE 1

CO 1 st.

Row 1: Kfb of that st (2 sts). Turn.

Row 2: Kfb, k1 (3 sts). Turn.

Row 3: Kfb, k2 (4 sts). Turn.

Row 4: Kfb, knit to end of row. Turn.

Repeat row 4 until you have 25 sts.

TRIANGLE 2

Row 1: Kfb, ssk. Turn.

Row 2 and all even rows: K.

Row 3: Kfb, k1, ssk. Turn.

Row 5: Kfb, k2, ssk. Turn.

Continue in this way, knitting one additional st between the kfb and ssk until you have worked all the sts from Triangle 1 (25 sts).

TRIANGLE 3

Row 1: Kfb, k2tog. Turn.

Row 2 and all even rows: K.

Row 3: Kfb, k1, k2tog. Turn.

Row 5: Kfb, k2, k2tog. Turn.

Continue in this way, knitting one additional st between the kfb and k2tog until you have worked all the sts from Triangle 2 (25 sts).

Repeat Triangles 2 and 3 until you have one small triangle and 11 large triangles for Silk Purse version, 15 large triangles for Silken Straw version.

Note

The Silk Purse version is worked with a single strand of yarn.

The Silken Straw version is worked with two strands of yarn held together throughout.

LAST TRIANGLE

Row 1: Kfb, k2tog. Turn.

Row 2 and all even rows: K.

Row 3: Kfb, k1, k2tog. Turn.

Row 5: Kfb, k2, k2tog. Turn.

Continue in this way, knitting one additional st between the kfb and ssk until you have 13 sts on the new triangle and 12 sts from the previous triangle.

Row 1: Ssk, k10, k2tog. Turn.

Row 2: Knit.

Row 3: Ssk, k9, k2tog. Turn.

Continue in this way, knitting one less st between the ssk and k2tog, until you have 3 sts, (2 sts from the new triangle and 1 st from the previous triangle.) Turn and K. Ssk, slip the last st from the left needle and pass the just-knit st over it. Break the yarn and pull through the last st.

FINISHING

Weave in ends.

the Connoisseur

by Gina Wilde & Lauren Lax

Paris provides the traveler with an experience in luxurious decadence. Art, music, entertainment, food, wine, fashion, history, and much more create a veritable Moving Feast. A place where adventure meets opportunity, Paris truly is the City of Love. Elegance is the dominant flavor of this French paradise— home to the quiet collector, the astute observer, and the seeker of things esoteric and subtle: the true Connoisseur.

The Connoisseur is the project of which such knit dreams are made. Incomparable softness and tactile ecstasy unite in this simple design, as Haiku and Silk Purse are stranded together on a fast needle to create the ultimate pullover. Work the two fibers in the same hue for subtle variegation in color, or select two different tones for a more dramatic 3-D color effect.

finished size

Chest: 32, (36, 40, 44, 48)"

materials

2 (3, 3, 4, 4) skeins
Alchemy Yarns Haiku
Shown in 26m – Platinum

4 (5, 5, 6, 6) skeins
Alchemy Yarns Silk Purse
Shown in 9c – Diamonda

US size 10 (6 mm) needles
(or size needed to obtain gauge)

US size 9 (5.5 mm) 16"
circular needles

Stitch holders

gauge

16 sts and 20 rows = 4"
in St st using larger needles
with one strand of each yarn held together

Seed Stitch

(worked on an even number of sts)
Row 1: *k1, p1, repeat from *
Row 2: *p1, k1, repeat from *

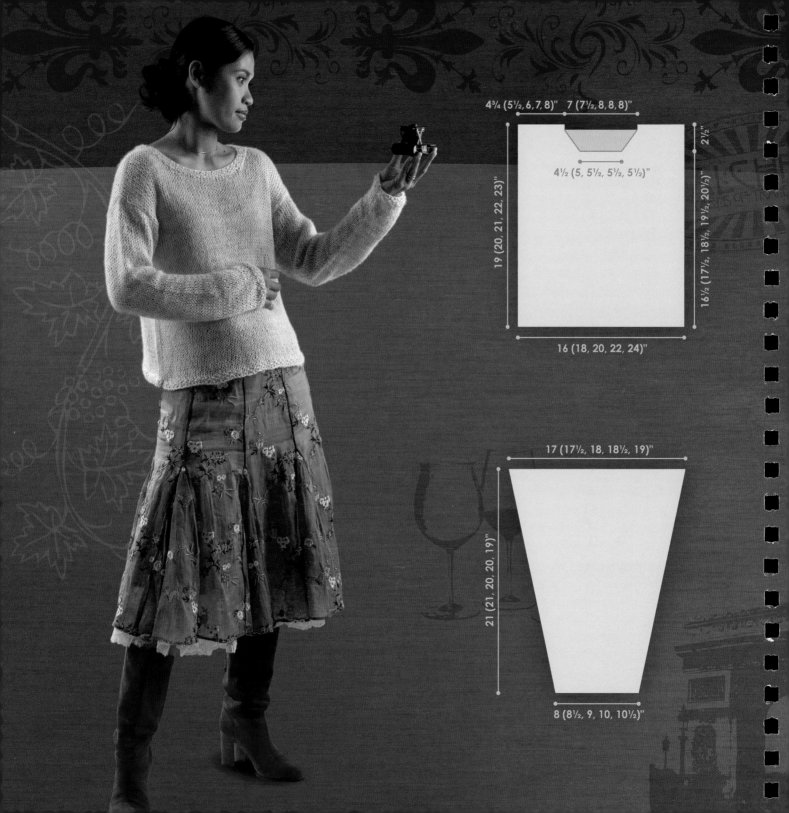

4¾ (5½, 6, 7, 8)"   7 (7½, 8, 8, 8)"

2½"

4½ (5, 5½, 5½, 5½)"

19 (20, 21, 22, 23)"

16½ (17½, 18½, 19½, 20½)"

16 (18, 20, 22, 24)"

17 (17½, 18, 18½, 19)"

21 (21, 20, 20, 19)"

8 (8½, 9, 10, 10½)"

Directions

BACK

With one strand of each fiber held together and larger needles, CO 66 (74, 82, 90, 98) sts. Work in Seed St for 1" for border. Change to St st and work until piece measures 19 (20, 21, 22, 23)" from beg, ending with a WS row.

Shape Neck: Knit 19 (22, 25, 29, 33) sts, join second ball of yarn (remember to strand the two fibers together) and BO center 28 (30, 32, 32, 32) sts, knit to end. Work 1 row (WS) and place rem sts on holders.

FRONT

With one strand of each fiber held together and larger needles, CO 66 (74, 82, 90, 98) sts. Work as for back until piece measures 16½ (17½, 18½, 19½, 20½)" from beg, ending with a WS row.

Shape Neck: Knit 24 (27, 30, 32, 34) sts, join second ball of yarn (remember to strand the two fibers together) and BO 18 (20, 22, 22, 22) sts, knit to end. Dec 1 st each side at neck edge every other row 5 times - 19 (22, 25, 29, 33) sts rem on each shoulder. Work even until same length as back to shoulders. Place rem sts on holders.

SLEEVES (MAKE TWO)

With one strand of each fiber held together and larger needles, CO 32 (34, 36, 40, 42) sts. Work in Seed St for 1". Working in St st, inc 1 st at beg and end of 7th and every following 4th row 6 (6, 6, 5, 5) times, then every 6th row 12 (12, 12, 12, 12) times - 68 (70, 72, 74, 76) sts. Work even until sleeve measures 21 (21, 20, 20, 19)" or desired length.

BO loosely.

FINISHING

Join front to back at shoulders using three needle bind-off.

Neckband: With smaller needle, pick up and knit 66, (70, 74, 76, 78) sts around neck edge. Work in Seed St for 1".

BO loosely in Seed St.

Sew sleeves to sides, matching center of sleeve with shoulder seam.

Sew side and sleeve seams.

Weave in ends.

Block lightly with steam on wrong side.

Moonlight Sonata Wrap

by Shelli Westcott & Marilyn Webster

Al chiaro di luna

Ludwig van Beethoven

The Piano Sonata Number 14 in C Sharp Minor, Quasi una Fantasia, is popularly known as the Moonlight Sonata. Dedicated to Beethoven's 17-year-old pupil, with whom it is rumored the great artist was once in love, it has been said of this piece that it "is one of those poems that human language does not know how to qualify." The stormy final movement reminds us of the beauty, sadness, and inevitable melancholy that are the exchange we receive when we give our hearts to love.

This classically elegant wrap is perfect for moonlit walks, summer strolls on the beach, or any time a touch of silken luxury is needed (isn't that all the time?) Embellished with a clever self-fringe and written with an option for including the delicate sparkle of beads (as shown), you'll make beautiful music in the Moonlight Sonata Wrap.

finished size

Silken Straw: approx 15" by 51"
Silk Purse: approx 20" by 60"
(measurements do not include fringe)

materials

1 skein Alchemy Yarns Silken Straw
Shown 67e – Topaz

US size 10½ (6.5 mm) needles
(or size needed to obtain gauge)

• • • or • • •

2 skeins Alchemy Yarns Silk Purse
Shown in 76e – Citrine

US size 11 (8 mm) needles
(or size needed to obtain gauge)

110 Beads
Be sure your beads have holes large enough to accommodate the yarn. We used 6mm Swarovski Crystal bicone beads.

Fine beading wire
or waxed dental floss

Stitch markers

gauge

Silken Straw:
15 sts and 16 rows = 4" in St st
(using US size 10½)

Silk Purse:
13 sts and 16 rows = 4" in St st
(using US size 11)

Note

These shawls are very flexible in terms of fiber and gauge. As shown, they are knit on large needles to create a loose fabric. If one prefers a tighter fabric, purchase another skein of yarn and use smaller needles.

CO 6 sts, leaving a 12" tail.

Row 1 (WS): P1, pm, k5.

Row 2 (RS): K5, sl marker, kfb (7 sts)

Row 3: P to marker, sl marker, k5.

Row 4: K5, sl marker, k1, m1, place bead, if desired, on next st, k to end.

Repeat rows 3–4 until there are 62 sts, ending with a WS row. *Note:* If you are using a different yarn, repeat rows 3–4 until you have used half your yarn.

Row 1 (RS): K5, sl marker, ssk, place bead, if desired, on next st, k to end.

Row 2 (WS): P to marker, sl marker, k5.

Repeat rows 1–2 until there are 7 sts, ending with a WS row.

Last row: K all the sts, sl the second to last st over the last st to bind off the last st. Cut thread leaving a 12" tail and pull through this st. Slide the remaining 5 sts off the needle *without binding off.*

FINISHING

The fringe is made by unraveling the 5 edge sts that were not bound off. Lay scarf on a flat surface and place a book or other weight on it. Unravel one garter ridge (two rows) at a time and tie a loose knot about ½" from the scarf. It is important not to tie the knot too close to the scarf. When all the rows have been unraveled, smooth scarf out and make sure that it lies flat. Tighten knots if desired. To work in the ends, fold each tail in half and tie a tight knot close to the scarf so that it looks like the rest of the fringe. If desired, cut the fringe.

Block lightly to size.

Working with Beads

Use either a piece of fine beading wire or waxed dental floss to make a bead threader. Fold your wire or floss so the short leg is approx 1/3 the total length and the long leg is approx 2/3. Place bead as follows: Put the fold of the threader through the bead until the short leg pops free. Slip the stitch from the needle and put the short leg of the threader through the stitch. Put the short leg back through the bead and push the bead down the threader onto the stitch. Remove the threader, slide stitch back onto left hand needle, and knit the stitch.

Silk Purse

A DK weight
pure silk single
with an inimitable glow.
Classically elegant
on its own, or mix with
Haiku for snuggle-
worthy luxury.

100% Silk

3
LIGHT

Approx 163 yards (148 m)
in a 50 gram skein

Recommended gauge:
22 sts = 4" on US size 6 needles

*To see the full range of luminous colors
available in Silk Purse, please visit our
website at* **www.alchemyyarns.com**

Très Très Chic Kerchief

by Gina Wilde

It's girls' night out.
The work week is done. Boyfriends,
husbands, and significant others
must fend for themselves as the
ladies get ready for a night on the
town. Finishing touches are applied,
as the sweet scent of anticipation
fills the air. Individual style is
the appropriate dress for evening
and, whether it's up or down,
the Très Très Chic Kerchief
makes a perfect accent.

Decadently satisfying Silk
is knit with a simple center miter
to create this most versatile piece.
Worn as a cravat, a sensational
kerchief over the head, or as a

finished size

At widest point: 36"

materials

1 skein Alchemy Yarns Silken Straw Shown in 85c – Desert Song

US size 5 (3.75 mm) needles
(or size needed to obtain gauge)

• • • **or** • • •

2 skeins Alchemy Yarns Silk Purse Shown in 09c – Diamonda

US size 7 (4.5 mm) needles
(or size needed to obtain gauge)

gauge

Silken Straw: 24 sts = 4" (on US size 5)
Silk Purse: 20 sts = 4" (on US size 7)

36"

12"

Notes

- *This reversible scarf is knit in one piece. 5 rows of Reverse St st alternate with 9 rows of St st. All the decs are worked on K rows.*

- *Dec row: K to 2 sts before marker, SSK, sl marker, K 1, sl marker, K2tog, K to end of row.*

- *The numbers are given for Silken Straw (Silk Purse).*

Directions

CO 183 (171) sts and work 4 rows in St st (K one row, P one row).

Next row (set-up row): K 91 (85), pm, K 1, pm, K 91 (85).

Section A: Work 5 rows in Reverse St st, beginning and ending with a knit row, and **AT THE SAME TIME**, dec as detailed in the Note *on every knit row.*

Section B: Work 9 rows in St st, beginning and ending with a knit row, and **AT THE SAME TIME**, dec as detailed in the Note *on every knit row.*

Alternate Sections A & B, working the dec row on every knit row, until 3 sts rem. BO.

FINISHING

Weave in ends. Block lightly to size if desired.

the Naturalist

by Lauren Lax

The great American wilderness, so vast and diverse, becomes a metaphor for witnessing the natural order of things and getting a sense of something bigger than ourselves—when we take in the view, we see everything a bit more clearly. From desert to sea, from mountain to plain, the naturalist need search no further to find the perfect destination for stirring the soul. As John Muir reminds us,

"When we try to pick out anything by itself, we find it hitched to everything else in the universe."

Devoted to beauty, and guided by texture and color, this simple cardigan celebrates the exquisite blend of two yarns. When Silk Purse joins Haiku, a sensuously soft fabric is created. Sophisticated depth of color is achieved by knitting two harmonious colorways together, resulting in a cardigan so organic and profound, you will truly feel part of the natural order of things.

finished size

Chest: 33 (36, 39, 42, 45, 48)" finished circumference

materials

5 (5, 5, 6, 7, 7) skeins Alchemy Yarns Silk Purse Shown in 53c – Forest Waltz

2 (3, 3, 4, 4, 4) skeins Alchemy Yarns Haiku Shown in 55c – Montreat Path

US size 10 (5 mm) needles *(or size needed to obtain gauge)*

US size 9 (4.5 mm) needles

7 buttons

Stitch marker

gauge

16 sts and 20 rows = 4" in St st on larger needles *with one strand of each yarn held together*

Note

This design is
worked in one piece
from the top down.

7½ (8, 8½, 9, 9½, 10½)"

8½ (8¾, 9, 9½, 10½, 10¾)"

14"

33 (36, 39, 42, 45, 48)"

Seed Stitch

(worked on an even number of sts)

Row 1: *k1, p1, repeat from *
Row 2: *p1, k1, repeat from *

Directions

YOKE

With larger needle, CO 38 (42, 48, 50, 50, 50) sts.

Set-up row (WS): P3, pm, p6 (7, 8, 9, 9, 9), pm, p20 (22, 26, 26, 26, 26), pm, p6 (7, 8, 9, 9, 9), pm, p3.

Row 1 (RS): K1, m1, *k until 1 st before marker, kfb, sl marker, kfb, repeat from * 3 times more, k to last st, m1, k1.

Row 2: Purl.

Repeat last two rows 4 (4, 4, 5, 5, 6) more times.

Row 3: CO 2 (3, 5, 5, 6, 7), *k to 1 st before marker, kfb, sl marker, kfb, repeat from * 3 times more, k to end.

Row 4: CO 2 (3, 5, 5, 6, 7), p to end – 100 (106, 116, 128, 130, 142) sts.

Row 5: *K to 1 st before marker, kfb, sl marker, kfb, repeat from * 3 times more, k to end.

Row 6: Purl

Repeat last two rows 13 (14, 15, 16, 17, 18) times more – 204 (218, 236, 256, 266, 286) sts.

Divide for lower body and sleeves: K to first marker – 29 (31, 34, 37, 38, 41) sts, place next 44 (47, 50, 55, 57, 61) sts on waste yarn for right sleeve, CO 4 (5, 5, 6, 7, 7) sts, pm, CO 4 (5, 5, 6, 7, 7) sts, k to next marker - 58 (62, 68, 72, 76, 82) sts, place next 44 (47, 50, 55, 57, 61) sts on waste yarn for left sleeve, CO 4 (5, 5, 6, 7, 7) sts, pm, CO 4 (5, 5, 6, 7, 7) sts, k rem 29 (31, 34, 37, 38, 41) sts.

LOWER BODY

There are now 132 (144, 156, 170, 180 ,192) sts. Work in St st without shaping for 15 rows.

Next row (Dec row - RS): K to 3 sts before marker, ssk, k1, sl marker, k1, k2tog, k to 3 sts before marker, ssk, k1, sl marker, k1, k2tog, k to end.

Repeat dec row every 4th row 3 times more. Work even for 9 (11, 11, 13, 13, 13) rows.

Next row (Inc row - RS): K to 1 st before marker, m1, k1, sl marker, k1, m1, k to 1 sts before marker, m1, k1, sl marker, k1, m1, k to end.

Repeat inc row every 6th row 3 more times. Work even in St st until piece measures 13" from armhole, or 1" less than desired length, ending with a RS row. Change to smaller needles and work in seed st for 5 rows. BO loosely in seed st.

SLEEVES

Move sleeve sts to smaller needle.

Using larger needle, CO 4 (5, 5, 6, 7, 7) sts, k sleeve sts onto larger needle, CO 4 (5, 5, 6, 7, 7) sts – 52 (57, 60, 67, 71, 75) sts. Dec 1 st at beg and end of every 8th row 9 (6, 6, 0, 0, 0) times, then every 6th row 0 (5, 6, 14, 15, 16) times – 34 (35, 36, 38, 41, 43) sts. Cont without shaping until sleeve measures 1" less than desired length. Change to smaller needles and work in seed st for 5 rows. BO loosely in Seed St.

Repeat for second sleeve.

FINISHING

With a cool iron, steam-press lightly on wrong side using a pressing cloth.

Neck band: With smaller needles and RS facing, pick up and knit 48 (56, 64, 66, 66, 66) sts evenly around CO edge at neck. Work in Seed St for 5 rows. BO loosely in Seed St.

Button band: With smaller needles and RS facing, pick up and knit 90 (92, 94, 96, 98, 102) sts along left front. Work in Seed St for 5 rows. BO sts loosely in Seed St.

Buttonhole band: With smaller needles and RS facing, pick up and knit 90 (92, 94, 96, 98, 102) sts along right front edge. Work in Seed St for 2 rows.

Next row (Buttonhole row): Work 2 (3, 4, 2, 3, 2) st in seed st, * yo, K2tog, work 12 (12, 12, 13, 13, 14) in seed st, repeat from * 5 times more, yo, K2tog, work 2 (3, 4, 2, 3, 2) in seed st. Work in Seed St for 2 more rows. BO loosely in Seed St.

Sew sleeve seams and underarm seams. Sew buttons opposite buttonholes.

Weave in ends.

Encantada Wrap

by Carolyn DesChamp

Barcelona gives architectural and artistic voice to the attitude of "anything goes." A wonderful example of Old World European grace uniting with New World Universal cool, Barcelona is a city where the Barri Gòtic of Medieval times literally shares a corner with an Andy Warhol exhibit.

A Symphony of extraordinary experiences constitute this phenomenal Catalonian capital of tolerance—from the Mediterranean-held tip of the quaint fishing village of Barceloneta, to the vista of Gaudí's Park Güell high above the city, and every colorful square foot in between, Barcelona is, quite simply, paradise.

So goes the Encantada, a knit interpretation of this favored destination. Simple lace equals eloquent grace in this architectural wrap. Alchemy's Haiku fiber is an exercise in luxurious softness, while the delicate finished fabric is wonderfully soothing against the skin.

ASSOCIATED DENTISTS
4506 REGENT ST
MADISON, WI 53705
[608]238-7112

Sale

ID: 76072298   Ref #:   0010
06/02/08   11:45:40
Batch #: 057

VISA

xxxxxxxxxx6658

Appr Code: 001241   Invoice#: 018998

Total $ 125.48

Approx 16" x 60"

2 skeins
Alchemy Yarns Haiku
Shown in 60a – Amethyst

US size 7 (4.5 mm) needles
(or size needed to obtain gauge)

Tapestry needle

16 sts = 4" in Lace Pattern Stitch
after blocking

Lace Pattern

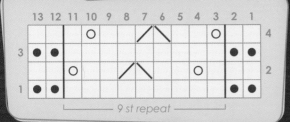

Note: The lace pattern is a multiple of nine sts plus four sts. To vary the width, add or subtract multiples of nine sts.

Directions

Loosely CO 67 sts. Knit 2 rows.

Row 1 (WS): K2, purl to last two sts, k2.

Row 2: K2, * k1, yo, k2, ssk, k2tog, k2, yo, repeat from * to last 2 sts, k2.

Row 3: K2, purl to last two sts, k2.

Row 4: K2, * yo, k2, ssk, k2tog, k2, yo, k1, repeat from * to last 2 sts, k2.

Repeat rows 1–4 until wrap is as long as desired, ending with row 4. Knit 2 rows.

BO loosely.

FINISHING

Weave in ends. Block to size. Don't hesitate to really stretch the lace in blocking. The more the lace opens up, the more beautiful it is.

Destination Alchemy

Queen of Hearts

by Gina Wilde

Ready... Steady... Go!

Time travel to Mod London during the late 50s and early 60s, where middle-class kids blended the garment trade with modern jazz and American rock and roll. Frequenting clubs like The Flamingo and The Scene, all night marauders took to the streets on Vespas in fine Italian suits and quiff hairstyles, pushing the edges of fashion and freedom.

Queen of Hearts rides alongside, made in one simple piece, minimizing the need for sewing seams. This timeless bolero knit in Silk Purse celebrates color and texture. Seed stitch and ruffles make a cuff suitable for a dandy.

finished size

Chest: 32 (36, 40, 44, 48)"

materials

5 (6, 7, 8, 9) skeins
Alchemy Yarns Silk Purse
Shown in 54w – Aquamarine

US size 5 (3.75 mm) needles
(or size needed to obtain gauge)

Size E crochet hook

Stitch holders

Tapestry needle

gauge

20 sts and 36 rows = 4"
in Seed Stitch

22 sts and 28 rows = 4"
in Stockinette Stitch

Seed Stitch (Odd)

(worked on ODD number of sts):
All rows: *K1, p1,
repeat from * to last st, k1.

Seed Stitch (Even)

(worked on an EVEN number of sts)
Row 1: *k1, p1, repeat from * to end.
Row 2: *p1, k1, repeat from * to end.

the *Patterns*

the *Fibers*

Destination...

Destination brings forth associations of travel—the call to explore something new, the knowledge that one is destined for a particular place, and the glorious sightseeing along the way. In order to arrive at a destination, one must experience a journey. This book is a map to guide you on a delightful knitting adventure, traveling through the land of noble fiber, exquisite hand paint yarns, and classic knit patterns to fill your heart and your hands.

Realizing there are many kinds of knitters (we are, after all, complex people), I don't want to oversimplify our lot with general classification of our unique fiber tendencies. But in my many years of being a fiber artist and encountering other needle art devotees, I hear over and again about two creative types: process knitters and product knitters. Some needle wielders are not so intent on the destination, as it were. They are along for the knit trip. It's all about the journey, and the process of enjoying one's creativity as it unfolds, without much concern with finished product. Instead, the goal is to enjoy simple shapes, glorious color, and the contemplative act of looping a simple string in myriad ways to realize something hand knit. Then there are those whose eyes are really trained on the prize; they might enjoy small needles, endless charts, elaborate shaping, or impressive knit gymnastics. Those are the product knitters (or the mathematically oriented, at the very least), and the creative process may be a by-product of their focus on the destination.

Personally, I am somewhere in between, with a foot in each camp. I want my process in the spotlight always, and

Directions

BACK

CO 63 (75, 87, 99, 111) sts. Work in Seed st for 20 rows, ending with a WS row.

Next row (RS): K, inc 9 sts evenly spaced across row – 72 (84, 96, 108, 120) sts.

Work in St st, increasing 1 st at beg and end of every other row 4 times, then every row 8 times, ending with a WS row – 96 (108, 120, 132, 144) sts.

Shape Sleeves: CO 2 sts at beg of next 12 rows, then CO 3 sts at beg of next 28 rows – 204 (216, 228, 240, 252) sts. Cont without shaping for 39 (39, 43, 43, 47) rows, about 4½ (4½, 5, 5, 5½)" above last CO edges for sleeves, ending with a WS row. Mark each end of last row for middle of sleeve.

Divide for Neck: K 86 (92, 98, 104, 110) sts, slip these sts onto holder for right front, BO 32 sts for back of neck, k to end of row.

LEFT FRONT

Row 1 (WS): P 71 (77, 83, 89, 95) sts, then work 15 sts in Seed st (center border).

Row 2 (RS): Work 15 sts in Seed St, k 71 (77, 83, 89, 95) sts.

Row 3: Repeat row 1.

Shape Neck: Next row (RS): Work 15 sts in Seed St, kfb, knit to end.

Keeping center front border in Seed St, continue in St st for 3 more rows, ending at center front edge.

Next Row (Short row): Work border, turn, sl 1, work Seed St to end.

Next row (Inc row): Work border, kfb, knit to end.

Repeat inc row every 4th row 3 (3, 4, 4, 5) times, then every other row 9 times AND AT THE SAME TIME repeat short row in border after every 8th complete row - 100 (106, 113, 119, 126) sts, ending at sleeve edge.

Notes

- The shrug is knit in one piece, starting at the lower back and working over the shoulders and down the front.

- Short rows are used to shape the curved front border.

Shape Sleeve: BO 3 sts at beg of next WS row. Cont to work short rows as above, and inc at neck edge every other row 14 times more **AND AT THE SAME TIME,** BO 3 sts at beg of every WS row 13 times more, then BO 2 sts at beg of next WS row, ending at center front edge – 70 (76, 83, 89, 96) sts.

Shape Border: Row 1 (RS): Work Seed st on 12 sts, turn.

Rows 2, 4, 6, 8 (WS): Sl 1, work Seed st to end of row.

Row 3: Work Seed st on 9 sts, turn.

Row 5: Work Seed st on 6 sts, turn.

Row 7: Work Seed st on 3 sts, turn.

Row 9: Work Seed st on 15 sts, work to end of row – 70 (76, 83, 89, 96) sts.

Row 10: BO 2 sts at beg of sleeve edge, work to end of row.

Row 11: Work Seed st on 3 sts, turn.

Row 12, 14, 16: Sl 1, work Seed st to end of row.

Row 13: Work Seed st on 6 sts, turn.

Row 15: Work Seed st on 9 sts, turn.

Row 17: Work Seed st on 12 sts, turn.

Row 18: Sl 1, work Seed st to end of row.

Next row: Work Seed st on 15 sts, place these border sts on holder, dec 1 st at center front edge, work to end of row.

Cont in St st only, BO 2 sts at beg of sleeve edge 4 times, then dec 1 st at sleeve edge every row 9 times, then every other row 3 times; **AND AT THE SAME TIME,** dec 1 st at center front edge every other row

6 times, then every row 12 times. BO rem 14 (20, 27, 33, 40) sts.

Replace border sts on needle, and cont working in Seed st until border is long enough to fit around shaped and lower edge of front to side edge. BO in Seed st.

RIGHT FRONT

Replace held sts on needle and reattach yarn at neck edge.

Rows 1 and 3 (WS): Work Seed st on 15 sts (center border), purl to end.

Rows 2 and 4 (RS): K to last 15 sts, work Seed st on 15 sts.

Shape neck: Next Row (WS): Work Seed st on 15 sts, kfb, purl to end.

Keeping center front border in Seed St, continue in St st for 3 rows more, ending at center front edge. Beg with short rows, work as for left front, reversing all shaping.

FINISHING

Cuffs: On RS of work, pick up and knit 43 (47, 51, 53, 57) sts around sleeve edge. Work in Seed st for 20 rows. BO in Seed st.

Sew front bands to lower front edge. Sew side and sleeve seams.

Cuff edging: With crochet hook, work 2 rows of single crochet around the cuff.

Next row: Work 2 sc in each sc of previous row.

Next row: Work 2 sc in each sc of previous row. Fasten off.

Neck edging: With crochet hook and right side of work facing, and starting at lower right hand corner, work edging as for cuffs.

Weave in ends. We recommended you avoid blocking this piece to prevent flattening the stitch texture.

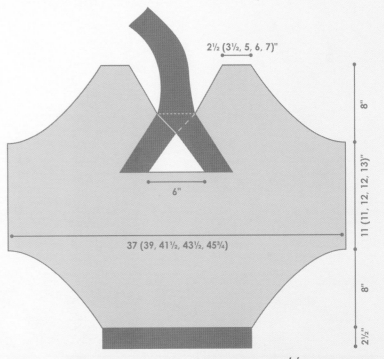

2½ (3½, 5, 6, 7)"

6"

37 (39, 41½, 43½, 45¾)

8"

11 (11, 12, 12, 13)"

8"

2½"

Around the World Ascot

by Gina Wilde

Up, up and away!

Take to the skies in a beautiful hot air balloon. Floating in thin air high above the hills and valleys, farmhouses and orchards look like miniatures below. Feel as free as a bird among the clouds, and witness the dawn of day from this rare perspective. It truly brings you a little bit closer to heaven.

Elegance is the signature of the sporty Silken Straw ascot. Worked in simple garter stitch, the intuitive shaping and inventive slip tie make an unforgettable accessory. Make this wonderfully draped piece in semi-solid colors (as shown) or work it up in a subtle and satisfying colorway.

finished size

Approx 5" x 30"
(from point to point)

materials

1 skein in each of two colors Alchemy Yarns Silken Straw Shown in 32e – Fig (MC) and 23e – Good Earth (CC)

US size 3 (3.25 mm) needles
(or size needed to obtain gauge)

Stitch holders

gauge

28 sts and 40 rows = 4" in Garter Stitch
(gauge is not critical in this piece)

Note

If this design is knit in one color, only one skein is needed. If the two color version is made, as shown in the photograph, there is ample yarn to make two ascots as long as the Main Color and Contrast Color are switched.

Directions

With MC, CO 3 sts.

Row 1 (WS): K.

Row 2 (RS): K1, Kfb, k1.

Row 3: K.

Row 4: K1, Kfb, k to end.

Repeat rows 3–4 until there are 34 sts. Work even in Garter St for 15".

Slash:

Next row (RS): *K1, sl next st onto holder, repeat from * to end.

Work the 17 sts rem on needle in K1, P1 rib for 2". Place these sts on holder, and break yarn. Replace 17 sts from first holder onto needle, reattach yarn, changing to CC if desired, and work in K1, P1 rib for 2".

Next row (RS): *K1 from holder, k1 from needle, repeat from * to end, returning sts to their original order.

Work even in Garter St for 1".

Row 1 (WS): K.

Row 2 (RS): K1, k2tog, k to end.

Repeat rows 1–2 until 3 sts rem. BO.

FINISHING

Weave in ends. Press lightly with a warm iron.

Abbreviations

Beg	Beginning		**Inc**	Increase(ing)
BO	Bind off		**K**	Knit
C6B	Slip next 3 stitches onto cable needle and hold at back of work, knit next 3 stitches from left-hand needle, then knit stitches from the cable needle		**K2tog**	Knit 2 stitches together
			Kfb	Knit in the front and the back of the next stitch – 1 st increased
			M 1	Make 1
C6F	Slip next 3 stitches onto cable needle and hold at front of work, knit next 3 stitches from left-hand needle, then knit stitches from the cable needle		**P**	Purl
			P2tog	Purl 2 stitches together
			PM	Place marker on needle
Ch	Chain		**PSSO**	Pass slipped stitch over
CN	Cable needle		**Rem**	Remaining
CO	Cast on		**RS**	Right Side
Cont	Continue(ing)		**Sc**	Single crochet
Dec	Decrease(ing)		**Sl**	Slip
Garter St	Knit every row		**SSK**	Slip, slip, knit
			St(s)	Stitch(es)
			St st	Stockinette Stitch: K the RS rows, P the WS rows
			Wyif	With yarn in front
			WS	Wrong Side
			YO	Yarn Over

Caring for Your Fine Handknits

Preserve your investment in fine natural fibers by taking proper care of your garments. While dry cleaning is generally a safe option, we prefer to gently hand wash Alchemy Yarns fibers at home.

Several of our designs include specific instruction for blocking. Following these instructions will give you the best combination of drape and dimensional stability.

Washing

Fill a sink or the tub of your washing machine with warm water and a bit of gentle detergent. Allow the garment to soak for a few minutes. DO NOT AGITATE. If you are concerned about a spot, gently squeeze and swish the soapy water through – DO NOT SCRUB or abrade the surface. Allow the sink or the tub to drain, gently pressing the garment against the side of the sink to remove excess water. Move the garment away from the water inlet, and fill the sink again with clear warm water. Gently swish and squeeze to rinse. Drain the sink again.

With your hands supporting the wet garment from underneath, lift it into a mesh laundry bag or a salad spinner. If you are using a mesh bag, take it outside, and then swing it around your head repeatedly to spin out the excess water. Think cowboy with a lasso. Yes, your neighbors will laugh. If this is too silly for you, use a big salad spinner to accomplish the same thing indoors without the overspray. If you are using your washing machine, and can control the action, use the spin cycle to remove the excess water. The objective is to remove as much water as possible while preventing stretch.

Take the now damp garment and lay it flat on a large table, spare bed, or un-trafficked spot of floor covered with a clean towel or old tablecloth. Gently pat, smooth and coax it into shape, paying special attention to edgings, collars and button bands. Leave the garment alone until it is thoroughly dry. This process will go faster if you choose a warm spot with good air circulation, or even turn on a fan if humidity is high.

Pressing

Give careful consideration to pressing your garment. Silken Straw loves a hot iron, and gentle pressing enhances the drape and softness of the fiber. With Haiku or Silk Purse, aggressive pressing can flatten the lovely texture of your garment. Usually, all that is needed is a bit of steam and a gentle patting and smoothing action to make your garment look perfect.

Storage

Do not hang your fine handknits. Doing so will invite unwanted stretching and leave hanger lumps in the shoulders. Neatly fold your garments and store in a snag-free drawer or closet shelf.

the *Designers*

M. Diane Brown

Diane has knit since she was a small child and began designing her own sweaters in the 1980s. Her work has appeared in the Jamieson's Shetland Knitting books and in Simply Shetland. She teaches knitting near her home in Northern California and is much in demand as a teacher of both traditional and contemporary knitting techniques.

Carolyn DesChamp

Carolyn DesChamp is a life long knitter who resides in southwestern Ontario, Canada. Over the years, she's enjoyed most knitting genres she's come across. Lace knitting has become a passion, particularly when that lace can be shown off with luxurious fibers and colors, as with her work with Alchemy yarns.

Lauren Lax

Lauren recently moved to the Bay Area, where she teaches math and statistics. After first learning to knit, she spent years working only with acrylics and scratchy wools. As a result, she feels fortunate to work with the luxury of Alchemy yarns.

Olga Pobedinskaya

Of Russian origin, Olga lived in England for 10 years before emigrating to America. She won First Prize in the British Hand-Knitting Council's knitting competition in 2004 and was a finalist in both 2005 and 2006. Olga took second place in the 2004 World's Fastest Knitter competition in London. Olga's original designs have sold to clients around the world. She can often be found behind the counter at the Knitting Tree in Madison, WI.

Sandi Rosner

Sandi taught herself to knit from the instructions in the back of a magazine in the late 1970s. She is the author of Not Just Socks, Not Just More Socks and Not Just Socks for Kids. Sandi designs for several yarn companies and teaches knitting design. She lives just a few miles from the Alchemy studio and is proud to be a long time friend of the Alchemy family.

Marilyn Webster

Marilyn's mother taught her to knit when she was six. Her passion for fiber arts includes weaving, spinning and a curiosity about global textile traditions. She began designing professionally during a stint working at Alchemy Yarns. Marilyn's work has recently appeared in Folk Style and her writing was featured in KnitLit the Third. She lives in Northern California.

Shelli Westcott

Before opening Knitterly, a stylish yarn shop in Petaluma, California, Shelli was a landscape designer. Her passion for the textures and colors provided by nature are now channeled into her love of all things yarn. She finds parallels as well between watching the growth of plants, watching the growth of a project and watching the growth of her customers in their skill as knitters. Her proudest creations are her two grown children.

Gina Wilde

In Gina's colorful career, she has been a sculptor, weaver, musician, studio arts teacher, performance artist, and arts administrator. Her work has appeared in Hand Knit Holidays, The Knitter's Book of Yarn, and Folk Style, as well as Vogue Knitting and Interweave Knits magazine. Her first book, Shibori Knits, will be published by Random House in 2008. She is the Creative and Artistic Director for Alchemy Yarns, holds a Masters Degree in Arts and Consciousness, and is a renowned speaker on the topics of color, knitting, and transformation.

Alchemy Stockists

Alchemy Yarns are available at fine independent yarn shops throughout the United States, Canada and Europe. The retailers listed below carry a wide variety of Alchemy fibers, including the specific yarns used to make the garments in this book. For more Alchemy Yarns retailers, please visit our website: www.alchemyyarns.com

Annie & Company
1325 Madison Ave., Gr. Floor
New York, NY 10128
(877) 289-5648
www.annieandco.com

Article Pract
5010 Telegraph Ave.
Oakland, CA 94609
(510) 595-7875
www.articlepract.com

Crazy for Ewe
22715 Washington St.
Leonardtown, MD 20650
(301) 475-2744
www.crazyforewe.com

Hill Country Weavers
1701 S. Congress Ave.
Austin, TX 78704
(512) 707-7396
www.hillcountryweavers.com

ImagiKnit
3897 18th St.
San Francisco, CA 94114
(415) 621-6642
www.imagiknit.com

Jessica Knits
10401 E. McDowell Mtn Ranch Rd #7
Scottsdale, AZ 85255
(480) 515-4454
www.jessicaknits.com

Knit Knack
1914 Springfield Ave.
Maplewood, NJ 07040
(973) 763-6066

Knit Stop
3941 E. 82nd St.
Indianapolis, IN 46240
(866) 763-0110
www.knit-stop.com

Knitterly
#1 4th St.
Petaluma, CA 94952
(707) 762-9276
www.knitterly.net

Knitting Arts
14554 Big Basin Way
Saratoga, CA 95070
(408) 867-5010
www.goknit.com

The Knitting Niche
115 Mason St.
Greenwich, CT 06830
(203) 869-6205
www.knittingniche.com

Knitty City
208 W. 79th St.
New York, NY 10024
(212) 787-5896
www.knittycity.com

Lettuce Knit
70 Nassau St.
Toronto, Ontario
M5T 1M5
(416) 203-9970
www.lettuceknit.com

Loop
1914 South St.
Philadelphia, PA 19146
(215) 893-9939
www.loopyarn.com

loop
41 Cross St.
Islington, London
N1 2BB, United Kingdom
020 7288 1160
www.loop.gb.com

Loops, A yarn store
2042 Utica Square
Tulsa, OK 74114
Toll-free (877) LOOPS-OK
www.loopsknitting.com

Purl
137 Sullivan St.
New York, NY 10012
(212) 420-8796
(800) 597-7875
www.purlsoho.com

Stash
1820 Solano Ave., Ste. B-2
Berkeley, CA 94707
(510) 558-YARN
www.stashyarn.com

Temptations
35 S. High St.
Dublin, OH 43017
(614) 734-0618
www.knit2temptations.com

Threadbear Fiber Arts Studio
319 S. Waverly Rd.
Lansing, MI 48917
(517) 703-9276
www.threadbearfiberarts.com

Unique One
2 Bayview St.
Camden, ME 04843
(888) 691-8358
www.uniqueone.com

Yarn Garden
1413 SE Hawthorne Blvd.
Portland, OR 97214
(503) 239-7950
www.yarngarden.net

Notes